AF873721

FACEBOOK 101

Let Your Customers Create Word of Mouth, Advertise Your Business, and Grow Your Sales

By Steve Weber
with Laurie Jackson

Published by Stephen W. Weber
Printed in the United States of America
Weber Books www.WeberBooks.com
ISBN: 978-1-936560-12-7

Acknowledgements

I'm indebted to each of these talented, hardworking people who helped make this book a reality in many ways:

Laurie Jackson, co-author. Laurie did most of the tough work of researching, double-checking, and illustrating this book.

Judy Corcoran, editor. Judy smoothed and polished the text.

Tim Hess, peer reviewer. Tim suggested numerous essential revisions to the draft.

Elaine Moertl, proofreader. Nobody beats Elaine when it comes to finding typos and other boo-boos.

—Steve Weber, author

Contents

INTRODUCTION: A NEW WAY TO CONNECT 7

In the beginning 7
Who's on Facebook… 8
… and what are they doing? 8
Eight ways to use Facebook to promote your business 10
1. Create a personal profile. 10
2. Join a group. 10
3. Start your own group. 10
4. Sponsor an event. 10
5. Create a Facebook Page. 10
6. Update your customers. 10
7. Buy ads. 10
8. Keep connected. 11

A TASTE OF SUCCESS WITH FACEBOOK 13

Crème-Delicious 13
The Gents Place 16
Woods Hole Inn 18
Inedible Jewelry 21

1 ► GETTING STARTED WITH FACEBOOK 25

Signing up for Facebook 25
The getting started page 28
View and Edit Your Profile. 28
Add a Profile Picture. 29
Facebook Pages 30
Facebook Ads 31
Facebook Platform 31

2 ► THE FACEBOOK HOME PAGE 33

Blue Menu Bar 33
Friends icon 34
Messages icon 34
Globe icon 34
Search 34
Profile 35
Find Friends 35
Home 35
Down-facing arrow 35
On the Left: Filters 35
In the Middle: Wall 36
- Friends icon 36
- Map Pin icon 36
- Globe icon 37

On the Right: Highlights 37
On the Bottom: Navigation Tools and Help 37

3 ▶ FINDING FRIENDS AND KEEPING CONNECTIONS 39

Invite a Friend by Email 40
Find Friends, Classmates and Coworkers 40
Search for people 41
Communicating Privately 41
Going public: Writing on a friend's Wall 42

4 ▶ BUILDING YOUR PROFILE 43

Choosing who sees what 43
Control your default privacy 44

5 ▶ SHARING PHOTOS 47

Uploading Photos 48
Editing and Tagging Photos 49
Viewing photos of yourself 49

6 ▶ JOINING OR STARTING A GROUP 51

Joining a group 51
Creating a group 52
Groups and market research 54

7 ▶ FACEBOOK PAGES 55

Groups vs. Pages: Which is better? 55
Who can create a Page? 56
Finding Pages and liking them 57
Creating a Page 58
Customizing your Page 59
Adding other information 62
About: 62
Photos: 62
Use Social Plug-ins: 63
Ready, set, publish! 63

8 ▶ PROMOTING AND MONITORING YOUR PAGE 65

Keep people coming back 66
Use your blog to promote your Facebook page… 67
...and vice versa 68
Use YouTube to promote your Facebook Page 68
Using Insights 68
A success story: the Rothbury Festival 72

9 ▶ FACEBOOK EVENTS 73

Finding and viewing Events 73
Create an Event 74
Step 1: Event Info 74
Step 2: Customize your event 75
Step 3: Invite Friends 75
Managing an Event 75
During an Event 76
After the Event 76
Success Story: Free Slurpee Day 76

10 ▶ PAID ADVERTISING ON FACEBOOK **79**

WILL PAID FACEBOOK ADS PAY OFF FOR YOUR BUSINESS? 80
GETTING STARTED WITH FACEBOOK ADS 80
WHY EXACTLY ARE PAID FACEBOOK ADS SO POWERFUL? 82
Everyone's on Facebook (almost). 82
Facebook Ads can be highly targeted. 82
Facebook ads complement your other marketing efforts 83
The effectiveness of Facebook ad campaigns is highly measurable. 83
Facebook ad campaigns aren't cheap, but they are affordable and very scalable. 84
STARTING YOUR FIRST CAMPAIGN 85
What is a Facebook Ad? 85
The difference between Standard Ads and Sponsored Stories: 86
Standard Ads 86
Sponsored Story Ads 87
LOGGING INTO THE AD MANAGER 88
THE AD CREATION PROCESS 89
SETTING UP YOUR AD OR SPONSORED STORY 89
Choosing your ad's "Facebook Destination or Outside URL": 89
TO CREATE A STANDARD AD 90
Choose your business's timeline or "place" page. 90
Enter a URL (web address) to an outside web page such as www.mysite.com. 90
TO CREATE A SPONSORED STORY AD 90
Choose "What You Want to Promote": 91
PROMOTING AN EVENT ON FACEBOOK 92
THE "PEOPLE WILL SEE" SELECTION 92
CRAFTING THE CONTENT OF YOUR AD 93
ART AND COPY: THE CREATIVE SIDE OF THE ADVERTISING WORLD 93
FACEBOOK AD COPY AND IMAGE DETAILS 94
Copy/text: 94
Images: 94
WRITE EFFECTIVE AD COPY 94
THREE SPECIFIC FACEBOOK AD COPY STRATEGIES 95
1. To raise awareness of your business or brand: 95
2. To highlight an outside piece of content. 95
3. To generate direct sales. 96
PICKING THE RIGHT IMAGE 96
CHOOSE YOUR AUDIENCE STEP 97
LOCATION 98
AGE AND SEX 99
INTERESTS 99
CONNECTIONS 100
ADVANCED TARGETING OPTIONS 100
EXAMPLES OF EFFECTIVE TARGETING 100
PAYING FOR, SCHEDULING, AND MONITORING YOUR AD 102
OBJECTIVES 102
SETTING YOUR BUDGET, PAYMENT METHOD, AND SCHEDULE 103
HEDGE YOUR ADVERTISING "BETS" 104
SPLIT TESTING: SCHEDULING ADS LIKE A MARKETING PRO 105
CAMPAIGN WRAP-UP AND GETTING IT POSTED 105
POST CAMPAIGN ANALYSIS AND THE AD MANAGER TOOL 106
THE AD MANAGER HOME PAGE 107
READING THE AUDIENCE PIE GRAPH 108

READING THE "RESPONSE" GRAPH 108
UNDERSTANDING THE CHART DATA 109
Pages tab: 109
Reports tab: 109
Advertising performance: 110
Responder demographics: 110
Conversions by impression: 110
Inline interactions: 110
Settings tab: 110
Billing tab: 111
Creative library: 111
Power editor tab: 111

11 ► FACEBOOK PLATFORM, OTHER APPLICATIONS 113

USING APPLICATIONS TO PROMOTE YOUR BUSINESS 113
ADVERTISING ON APPLICATIONS 114
ADDING APPS TO YOUR PAGE 114
OTHER FACEBOOK APPLICATIONS 116
FACEBOOK MOBILE: CONNECTING ON THE RUN 116
FACEBOOK NOTES: LETTING YOUR FRIENDS KNOW WHAT'S ON YOUR MIND 117
FACEBOOK MARKETPLACE, POWERED BY OODLE 118

INDEX 121

INTRODUCTION: A NEW WAY TO CONNECT

In just its first few years, Facebook has grown from a college dorm-room project to one of the most popular Internet destinations. The site is the second most frequently visited website, attracting millions of visitors each month. And, while Google currently ranks No. 1 in visitors, Facebook far outranks it in the amount of time spent using it. It has become the dominant force in a phenomenon it helped to create: online social networking.

Facebook appeals to a fundamental human need: connecting with other people. At its basic level, that is what social networking is all about. Facebook has become ubiquitous because it helps us make and keep connections. For example:

- Some of your best memories of high school involve playing on the varsity volleyball team. But somehow, over the years, you have lost touch with all your teammates. Facebook can help you reconnect.
- You move to a new city where you don't know a soul. That experience can be exhilarating but it can also be a little scary. Facebook can help you find people who share your interests.
- Your friends from college are spread out all over the country. You would like to keep them informed about what's going on in your life, and you would also like to know what's happening in theirs. Facebook is like an online class reunion—without the last-minute dieting.
- You've decided to launch a home-based business. You expect that your first customers will be friends, family and acquaintances. Facebook gives you a convenient way to tell everyone you know (and their friends) about your new venture.

It helps that Facebook is easy and fun to use. Signing up takes just a minute or so. Once you have signed up, you can easily search for friends or join an online community. You can also use Facebook to promote yourself or your business. That is the focus of this book.

But before we look at using Facebook for business purposes, let's see how this phenomenon started and where it seems to be heading.

In the beginning...

In 2003, Harvard sophomore Mark Zuckerberg embarked on a fairly sophomoric project. He hacked into Harvard's computer network and downloaded student identification photos of many of his fellow students. Then he placed two photos next to each other on a website and asked users to choose the "hotter" person. He called his site "Facemash."

The site became an instant hit on campus, but Harvard administrators were unhappy with Zuckerberg's project. They accused him of copyright violations, security breaches, and invading students' privacy. He even faced expulsion, but eventually the school dropped the charges. The next semester Zuckerberg launched "The Facebook," a photo directory of Harvard students. Within a month, half the student body had become members.

Colleges had been publishing "face books" of their students, especially freshmen, for years, but Zuckerberg was the first to put it all online. At first, access to the site was restricted to Harvard students, but in 2004 The Facebook expanded to include Stanford, Columbia and Yale. The expansion continued rapidly, and by 2005 membership was open to students at most U.S. and Canadian universities.

With membership growing exponentially, Zuckerberg moved his base of operations to Palo Alto, Calif., and bought the domain name "facebook.com" for $200,000. In 2005 Facebook opened membership to high school students, and by 2006 membership was open to anyone over the age of 13 with a valid email address. Today the site claims to have over 845 million active monthly users worldwide.

Who's on Facebook...

Since Facebook started on a college campus, many people assume that it is mainly for young people. While it is true that 70% of U.S. users are 25 or younger, the percentage of users in the 35+ age group is still growing. Almost 72% of all U.S. Internet users are now on Facebook; worldwide the number is one in every 13 people on earth, with over 250 million of them (that's more than 50%) who log in every day.

In the U.S., more women than men use Facebook, but beyond that, it's hard to pin down the demographics of Facebook members. For example, there is no data available on the ethnicity, income or politics of the entire Facebook membership. If, however, you decide to buy ads on Facebook, you can target your ads by age, gender, location, education and other variables.

In terms of promoting yourself or your business, the important thing to realize is that membership in Facebook is so huge that you will probably have no trouble finding a large target audience.

... and what are they doing?

Facebook users are constantly developing new ways to use the site, but make no mistake: Facebook has become more of a utility than a website. That is, people use Facebook the way they use their email accounts, checking daily and/or multiple times per day. Currently, the most common activities on Facebook are:

Connecting with friends: Facebook helps you track down people you have lost touch with. You can search for specific individuals or browse through the profiles of people in your networks (more on networks later). Once you have connected with a friend, you can find other people you may know by searching that person's list of friends.

Communicating with other Facebook users: Facebook provides an easy way to communicate with people you know (or people you have just met) without having to track down email addresses or phone numbers.

Posting photos: Facebook allows you to create and organize your own photo album. Instead of emailing individual photos to your friends, you can just direct them to your Facebook profile. You can link every photo you upload to the profiles of the people in the photo. For example, if you have a photo of yourself with your college roommates, you can link the photo to your roommates' profiles and it will appear there along with their other photos.

Tagging photos: A tag is a certain kind of link. You can tag a photo to reveal the names of the people in the photo. For example, you can post a status update and use tags to indicate who you're with. If you tag a friend in your status update, anyone who sees that update can click on your friend's name and go to their timeline. Your status update will also show up on that friend's timeline. (They can remove the link if they don't like the way they look.)

Joining groups: Groups are basically web pages devoted to a shared interest. For example, you might decide to join a group devoted to quilting or kayaking or skydiving. Groups also form to promote causes, such as Alzheimer's research. Depending on the group's settings, members can upload photos, receive messages, or check on news.

Liking pages: Businesses offer free goodies when you Like their page, and who doesn't like free stuff?

Planning events: Facebook provides a convenient way to inform people about events, such as conferences, parties or public meetings. People can easily RSVP and then receive reminders as the date for the event draws closer.

Using third-party applications: Software developers have created literally thousands of applications or "apps" that are available through Facebook. You can use third-party applications to play Scrabble, build your family tree, or take a personality test.

Promoting a business: Chances are, you're a fan of something or someone. You might be a fan of a particular writer or band or product. You probably have a favorite TV show or actor or political figure. What if businesses had a way of building on this kind of fan loyalty to promote their products or services? That is what Facebook offers—a new way of connecting with customers that is more powerful and less costly than conventional advertising.

Facebook offers three ways to promote your business:

- A **Facebook Page** is like a personal profile, with a few important differences. Unlike a profile, it gives you detailed insights about how people view and interact with your content.
- **Facebook Ads** take the concept of targeting specific audiences to a new level. You can define the audience for your ads by age, education, gender, interests and other variables. You can even tell people what their friends think of your products.
- **Facebook Platform** provides a way for you to build an application that will integrate your business with Facebook. This tool is not for everyone: It requires some expertise in web development. You can also advertise on existing applications without developing one of your own.

Eight ways to use Facebook to promote your business

Here are some examples of ways we'll explore using Facebook to promote your business. Although the following suggestions are in no particular order, we'll illustrate them throughout this book. After you have had a chance to experiment a little with Facebook, you will probably come with your own brilliant ideas on how to use it to promote your business.

1. **Create a personal profile.** You don't need to create a personal profile to advertise on Facebook, but if you don't, you won't have a real understanding of what Facebook is all about. You can't make the most of Facebook as a promotional tool if you don't understand how people use it.

2. **Join a group.** Groups are meeting places for people who share common interests. If you sell supplies for making jewelry, you could join one of the many groups devoted to jewelry making. Every group has a discussion board. You can eavesdrop on these discussions to find out what jewelry makers think about different products and what they're looking for. You can also join the discussion and let people know, in a low-key way, what you offer. Don't make your contribution to the discussion sound like an ad. People join groups to share information and opinions, not to be bombarded with ads. Keep in mind that when you join a group, its members cannot see any more of your information than they would otherwise. In other words, if you have privacy setting on your profile set to "Friends Only," group members who aren't your Friends won't be able to access your information.

3. **Start your own group.** If you can't find a group that is really relevant to your business, start your own group. Recruit your friends and loyal customers to become members.

4. **Sponsor an event.** Sponsoring an event can be a worthwhile promotional activity, even if you don't use the Events feature on Facebook to publicize it. Small businesses sponsor all sorts of events: fund raisers for nonprofit organizations, instructional workshops for customers, open houses. Events like these get your name in front of the public and attract people to your business. By using the Events feature on Facebook, you can announce your event to a wider audience and keep a record of who plans to attend.

5. **Create a Facebook Page.** A Facebook Page is like a free website. It doesn't give you the flexibility of a website in terms of appearance, but it is an effective way to create a presence on the web at no cost. You can use your page to tell people about your business, announce upcoming events, and provide basic information about your location and hours of operation.

6. **Update your customers.** If you have a Facebook page, you can use it to send updates to your fans about anything new that is happening in your business. You might send updates about a new product line or a new item on your restaurant's menu. Just be careful not to send updates too often. If fans get tired of seeing your updates, they can easily block them.

7. **Buy ads.** Advertising on Facebook offers several advantages. You can easily define a target audience by age, gender, location and interests. You can mount an ad campaign on a very modest budget, and you can set a limit on how much you will spend on advertising each day. You can see detailed reports on how people are responding to your ads. And finally, you can add a "social" element to your ads that will allow people to see if their friends have become fans of your business.

8. **Keep connected.** If you have a website, you know that the best way to keep people coming back is to give them something new to look at. The same is true for Facebook. If you have a Facebook page, post on your wall frequently. Use the events section of your page to let people know what you have coming up. Send updates to your fans whenever you have something interesting to announce. If you belong to a group, contribute to the discussion board frequently, and pay attention to what other people are saying. If you have a personal profile, keep connected with your friends. That's what Facebook is really all about.

A TASTE OF SUCCESS WITH FACEBOOK

In this section, we'll meet four entrepreneurs who have used Facebook to expand their businesses. Each has used different methods for generating organic, grassroots publicity and, in some cases, have used Facebook paid advertising to extend their reach. Although each of their businesses are different, and their marketing approaches vary, they've all found Facebook to be a vital tool for getting new clients, making more sales, and keeping their customers involved.

Crème-Delicious

Sandy Patangay is the founder, designer, artist, and marketing guru behind Crème-Delicious Inc., a New York cake boutique offering exquisite, hand-decorated artisanal cakes. A relative newcomer without a brick-and-mortar retail outlet, Sandy has concentrated on using Facebook to funnel customers to the Crème-Delicious website, where they can find more product information and place orders.

Question: How did you get into the cake business?

I worked on Wall Street for several years, and on the weekends I practiced Henna artistry—body art is part of my culture. Many people who saw my body-art designs suggested I could be a wonderful cake decorator. So one day out of curiosity, I bought a cake, decorated it, and took a photo. That photo was shown on a food blog, and all of a sudden, people wanted to know about my "cake line." So I decided to launch a henna-inspired cake line.

Would a business such as this, without a storefront, be possible before the Internet?

Yes, but it would take much longer. People would experience my cakes, and some of them would spread the word locally. But with the Internet, I can find customers on the other side of the planet!

Question: How did you get started with Facebook?

When my first cake was seen on that blog, I started getting emails asking for product information. I didn't have a website yet, and that took another five or six weeks. So I quickly launched a Facebook Page, uploaded a few images with product details, and began taking orders.

What Facebook techniques have proved the most effective for you?

Simply keeping our fans aware of what's new at Crème Delicious. I do one or two posts per week, and upload at least one image so fans see a new cake design on their Wall. This encourages their family and friends to check us out on Facebook and perhaps place an order.

It's very interactive—I ask fans for their suggestions and feedback. I listen to them, and they feel like they are really a key to our success.

Can you share more tips for spreading the word on Facebook?

Be Liked or get on the Facebook Wall of big names in your line of business. For example, we're friends with Brides Magazine and Ron Ben Isreal, the cake designer who hosts a Food Network show. People who visit them on Facebook discover our page, too.

Also, we participate in contests, giveaways and charity events. This brings attention, and some people end up buying our cakes because they've noticed something unique and fun.

Have you tried paid advertising through Facebook?

I have looked into it, but haven't tried it yet.

Beyond Facebook, what other publicity techniques have you tried?

Every week I reach out to food writers, magazine editors, event planners, and foodie and gift-oriented websites. For those in New York, we'll deliver free samples before the holiday season to encourage them to feature us as a potential holiday gift. In turn, these things bring traffic to our Facebook Page and website.

The Gents Place

Ben Davis, the 29-year-old founder of The Gents Place, a Dallas-based chain of high-end barbershops, had an idea for attracting customers with Facebook. It's a generous offer: a haircut, shampoo and hot towel treatment worth $35—absolutely free for clients who register their name, email address and phone number through Davis' Facebook Page. It's working, too! He's signed up 5,000 clients through Facebook for an average cost of $10 per new client. The payoff comes when some of those new Facebook clients eventually buy annual memberships worth $595 or more, which provides a haircut every two weeks, a 60-minute massage every month, and other extras like scalp massages and shaves.

Question: How do you attract customers using Facebook?

We have a "free trial haircut service" offer that we publicize mainly with Facebook advertisements. We ask prospects to Like our Page and register in exchange for a free first visit worth $35 to $45.

First, we created a custom app for the Facebook Page that drives Likes in exchange for the free haircut service. This is sometimes called "Like gating." Secondly, we allow the user to "share" the offer with their Facebook friends after they've completed the signup form. So this helps make the offer "go viral" and drives more Likes.

Third, we run monthly Facebook polls for our users and offer a free gift in exchange for completing the poll. Fourth, we include social media icons on all our email correspondence with our clients.

So your Facebook ads are definitely working. What about the free, grassroots techniques available?

Yes, we are very aggressive on Facebook's paid advertising platform. It's been extremely effective for us because we have a fairly low acquisition cost, about $10, to drive someone into the store. Then we have a good chance of converting them into a member.

The grassroots techniques add value to our overall marketing strategy, but I have limits on how much time I spend pursuing these—no more than two or three hours per week. You can get sucked into the vortex of Facebook surfing. Even though it is free, it has a real opportunity cost in terms of my time.

How do your results from Facebook compare to other social media or traditional marketing?

Overall, we have found Facebook to have the best return on investment. On Facebook, you aren't competing for high-demand keywords, which can happen with Google Adwords. So we've found that our cost-per-click is much lower on Facebook compared to search engines, where costs are prohibitive.

Although LinkedIn would appear to be where most of our clients are, Facebook still performs better because it allows more ad content, like a compelling photo, plus granular targeting—down to the level of Zip Code, Likes, interests, etc. By contrast, LinkedIn only allows targeting to the DMA level, which makes it difficult to drive business to a highly localized small business.

Woods Hole Inn

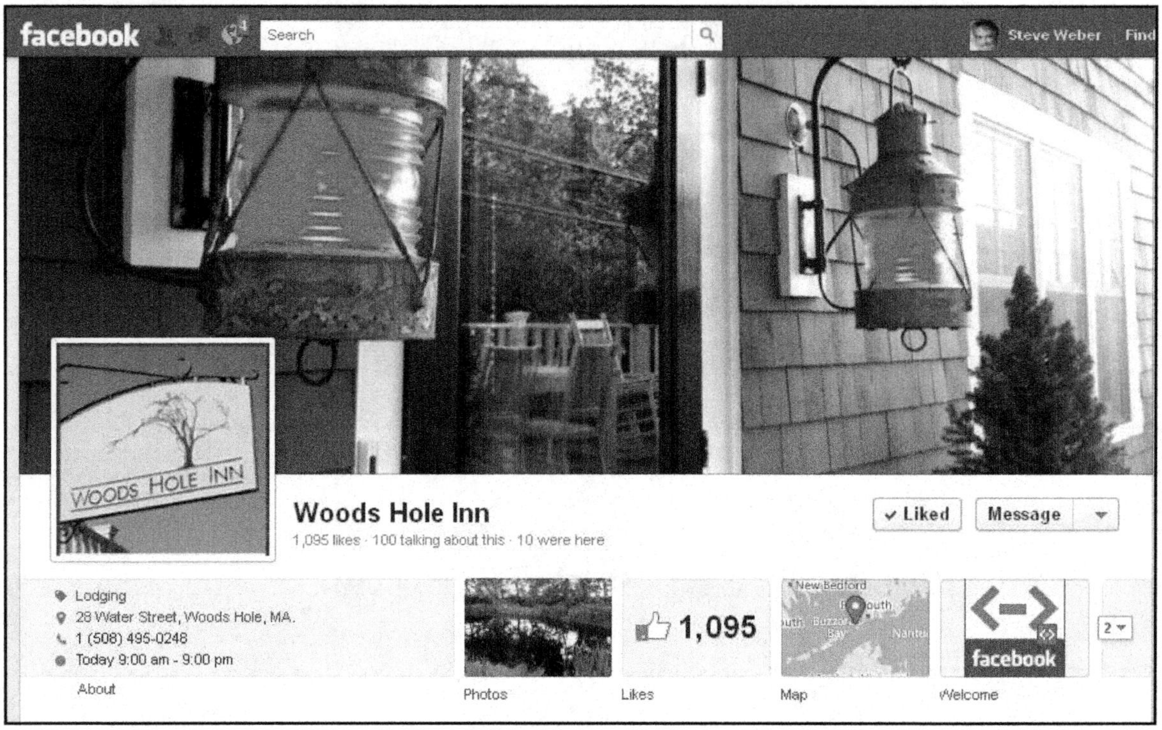

Innkeeper Beth Colt has used grassroots Facebook publicity to promote her newly restored Woods Hole Inn near Cape Cod, Mass. From the start, she methodically posted snapshots of her inn and its surrounding scenery to her Facebook Page. Last year one of her photos went viral, helping thousands of prospects from around the globe discover Woods Hole, without a dime in advertising fees.

Question: How did you get started?

After we moved here, I made several trips to a "swap shop" where you can find gently used furniture and other stuff. One day I found a red wooden chair that looked perfect for our new porch.

In January, the pond behind our house froze, and we decided to go skating. I grabbed the red chair to help the kids get their skates on. As we left the pond that evening, I noticed we had forgotten the red chair. There it sat, alone on the frozen pond. I got out my handy iPhone and snapped a picture. The image of that red chair is a perfect metaphor, an invitation to come explore in a quiet and beautiful place.

Later that evening, I posted the picture on Facebook as part of my photo project I call "365"—I post a new picture every day. The red chair ignited my Facebook friends and fans. I'd never received so many comments. People were even asking for posters of the red chair.

In March I received an email from a prospective guest, a photographer from California named Julie Cromer. She'd seen the red chair photo on my Facebook page. She booked a weekend visit and asked if she could borrow the chair.

About two weeks after Julie's visit, a huge package arrived. She sent a print showing our beach, with the read chair sitting in front of the crashing waves—a breathtaking picture. I hung the print in a prominent place at the inn, by our guest water cooler.

What happened next?

I decided to share the chair. I sent it on a first-class trip around Cape Cod and the islands. I called up the best inns and the finest bed-and-breakfasts, and asked them to show the chair around and photograph it participating in iconic Cape Cod activities—fishing, boating, even yoga. Each innkeeper lent their unique creativity. Now the photos are on Facebook and a website, RedChairTravels.com.

So you've really connected with your clientele through Facebook in a way that wasn't possible before?

I get a lot of feedback from Facebook and have definitely connected with my customers there. I have close "friendships" there with some of our regulars, and I always get a response when I post offers or availability openings. For example, if I get a last-minute summer cancellation, I post it on Facebook and it usually fills up. About 2,000 people are engaged with my brand via Facebook, so that's not too shabby for a 14-room property! Of course I would love to see it keep growing, so I work on it a lot.

What's next?

My plans are to send the chair to Nantucket, Martha's Vineyard and, eventually, to Santa Barbara, California, to visit Julie.

Inedible Jewelry

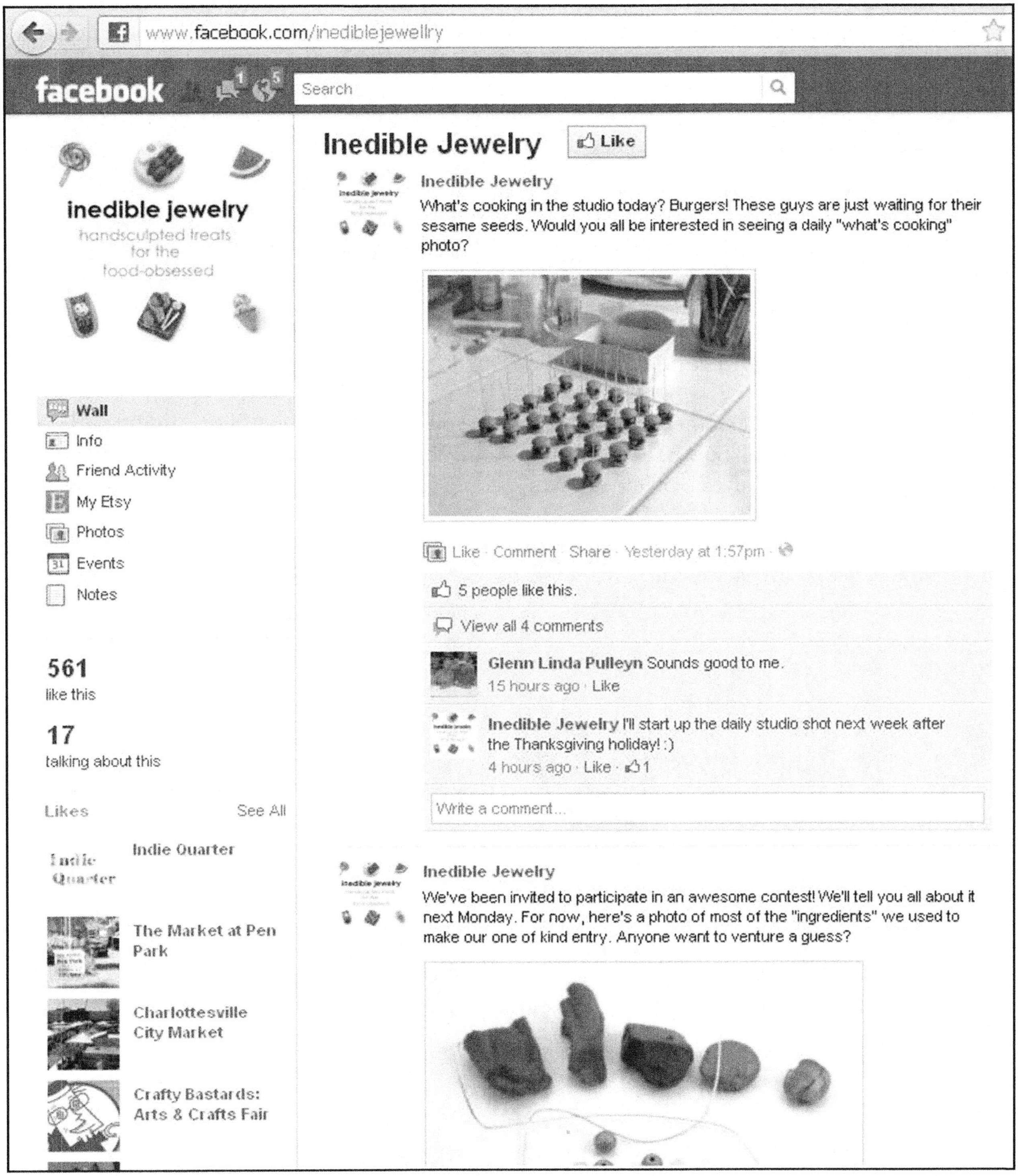

The Facebook Page for "Inedible Jewelry," which sells handmade food-themed jewelry like earrings, necklaces and cufflinks in the shape of hot dogs, cupcakes or perhaps a piece of pumpkin pie. Sisters Jessica and Susan Partain began sculpting and baking these tiny treats made from polymer clay as a fun hobby, but it's mushroomed into big business.

Question: How did you get started?

We began sculpting miniature food jewelry when we were kids, about 20 years ago. We started out creating dollhouse foods, then decided they'd be more fun as jewelry for people to wear, instead of static miniatures. In 2006 we started selling our work at local markets in Charlottesville, Virginia, and the business grew from there.

Where do you get new ideas?

We're both food-obsessed, so our creative process really boils down to investigating new foods. We're constantly brainstorming fun new designs. Our major limiting factor now is balancing our proven best-sellers with new designs. We read food blogs, chat with foodies on Twitter, cook real foods, and ask our customers what they want.

How do you find customers and repeat business?

Targeted marketing brings in customers. Our customers appreciate hand-made work, and food for that matter, and they tend to be playful. So we're on Facebook, and constantly networking with people who share similar interests. Everyone loves food, and playful people also like to wear their favorite foods!

We get repeat business by concentrating on great customer service, providing a fantastic quality product, and generally being upbeat and fun.

Jessica and Susan Partain greet customers at a craft show in Washington, D.C.

How big is your online business compared to shows and markets?

About a third of our business is shows and markets, about a third is online, and the other third is wholesale clients.

What's your advice about paying for advertising?

I honestly can't give direct advice because we've never paid for advertising. Online, our approach has focused on word of mouth—Facebook and Twitter have been huge assets—and carefully selected collaborations with other websites. We collaborate with high-profile blogs that target our market, but from a different angle. And we work hard on keywords and Search Engine Optimization. We've done some fun giveaways with foodie blogs, and that's gotten our name out there without advertising.

For those just getting started, I recommend spending some serious time figuring out your target market and learning Google Analytics. Before paying for any advertising, it's essential to understand where your traffic is coming from, and measuring your success with keywords. Without some baseline, it's impossible to know whether your advertising is effective or a waste of money.

1 ► GETTING STARTED WITH FACEBOOK

If you're just using Facebook to promote yourself or your organization, you don't necessarily need a personal account. But having your own Facebook account is a good idea for a couple of reasons. First, it helps you learn what Facebook is all about. The overwhelming majority of Facebook users are individuals, not businesses. Having a personal account lets you see what the Facebook experience is like for the people you want to reach.

Second, Facebook is fun. Just because you want to use Facebook for promotional purposes, that doesn't mean you can't enjoy all the other cool things it offers, such as keeping in touch with relatives, sharing photos, and telling all your friends about your latest amazing achievements.

If you're already intimately familiar with Facebook and are ready to begin applying it to your business, you might wish to skip directly to Chapter 7, Facebook Pages, and Chapter 10, Paid Advertising on Facebook.

Signing up for Facebook

Joining Facebook is fast and easy. All you need is a valid email address (an address that allows you to send and receive email).

Begin by going to Facebook.com. Fill in the information in these boxes:

- **Full Name:** Use your real full name. Do not use a phony name or alias. Facebook has controls in place to protect your privacy.
- **Your Email:** Enter the address where you would like to receive email.
- **Password:** Choose a password that is easy to remember but not obvious. Some people suggest using a password that is unique to Facebook and not one you use everywhere else.
- **Select Sex:** Choose male or female.
- **Birthday:** Enter your birth date. You can hide this information if you want.

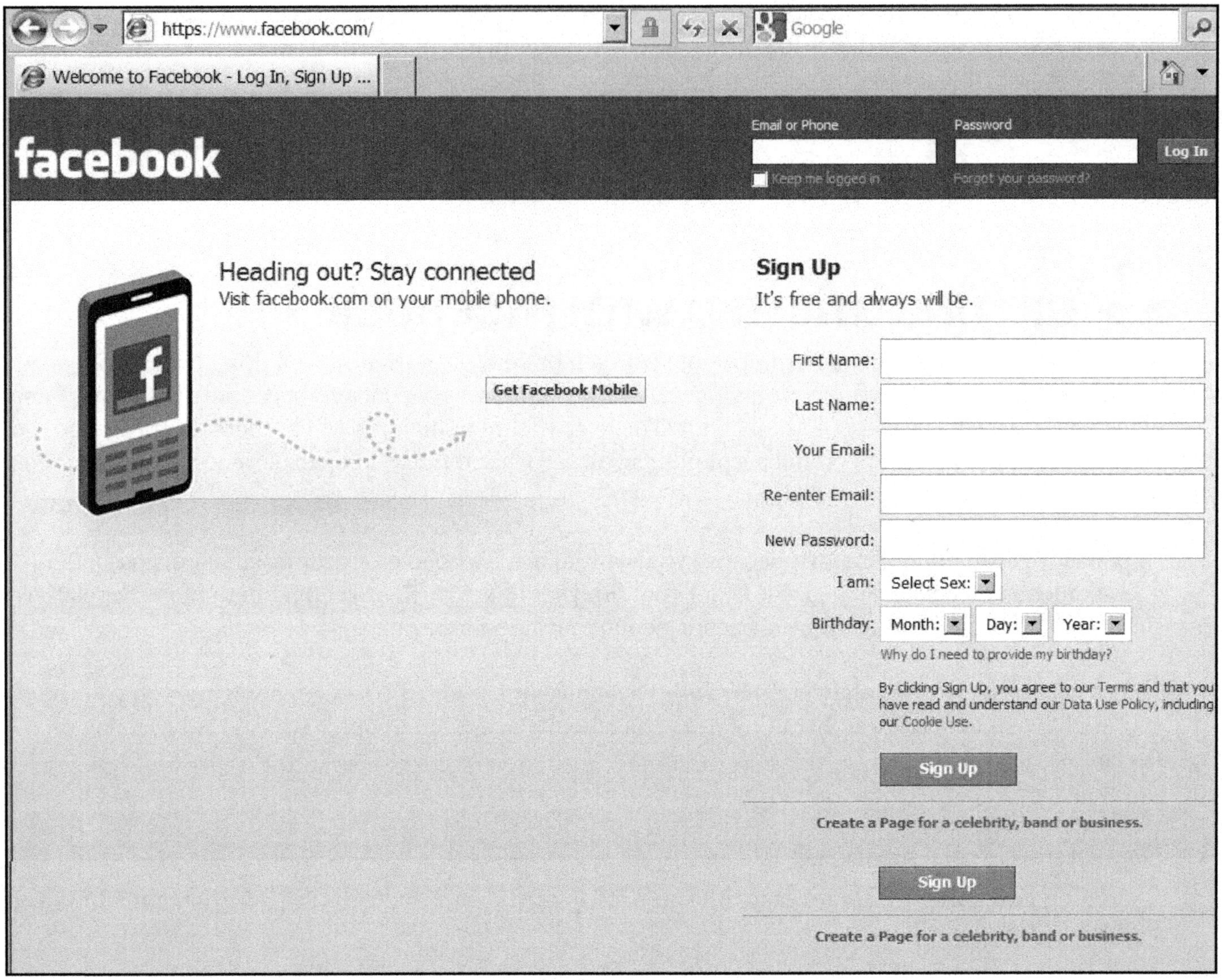

After you've entered this information, Facebook will congratulate you and tell you that a message confirming your registration has been sent to your email address. Go to your email, open this message, and click on the link. You will be taken to Facebook's "Getting Started" page.

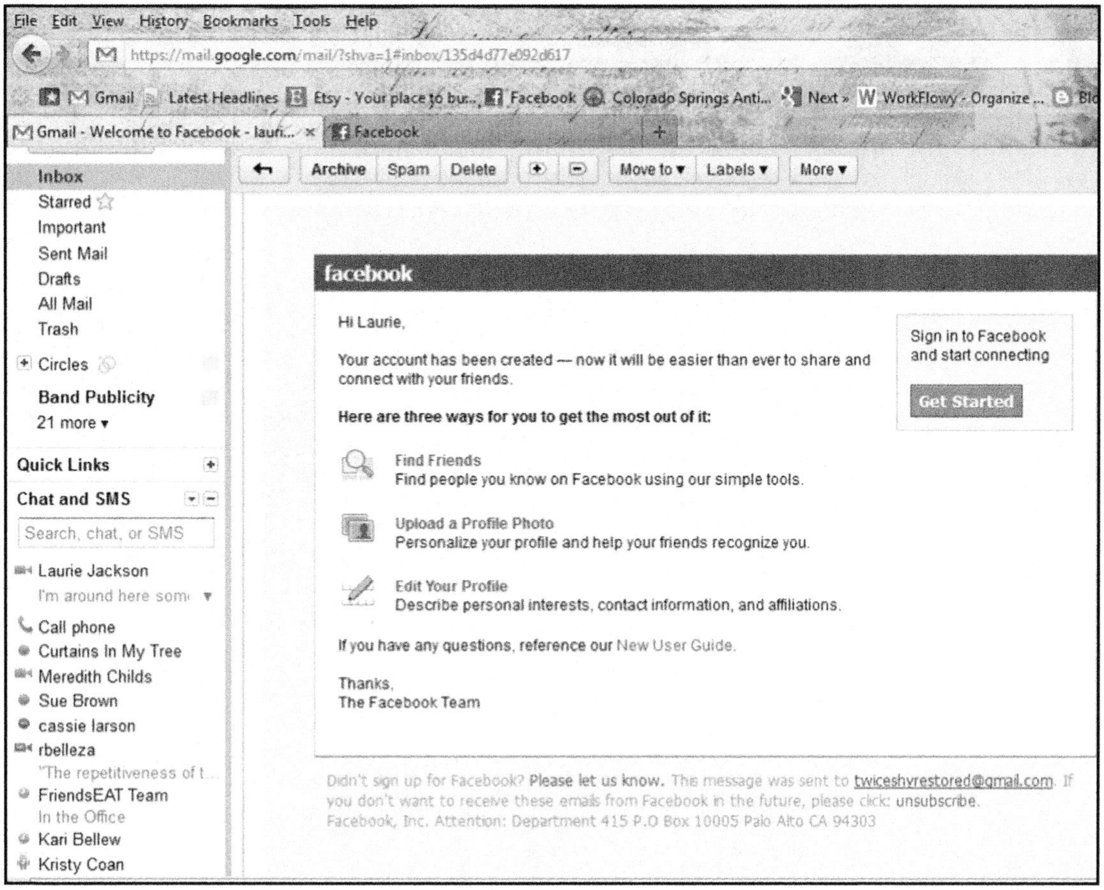
File Edit View History Bookmarks Tools Help
https://mail.google.com/mail/?shva=1#inbox/135d4d77e092d617
Gmail - Welcome to Facebook - laur...
Facebook
Inbox
Starred
Important
Sent Mail
Drafts
All Mail
Trash
Circles
Band Publicity
21 more
Quick Links
Chat and SMS
Search, chat, or SMS
Archive
Spam
Delete
Move to
Labels
More
facebook
Hi Laurie,
Your account has been created — now it will be easier than ever to share and connect with your friends.
Here are three ways for you to get the most out of it:
Find Friends
Find people you know on Facebook using our simple tools.
Upload a Profile Photo
Personalize your profile and help your friends recognize you.
Edit Your Profile
Describe personal interests, contact information, and affiliations.
If you have any questions, reference our New User Guide.
Thanks,
The Facebook Team
Sign in to Facebook and start connecting
Get Started
Didn't sign up for Facebook? Please let us know. This message was sent to twiceshyrestored@gmail.com. If you don't want to receive these emails from Facebook in the future, please click: unsubscribe.
Facebook, Inc. Attention: Department 415 P.O Box 10005 Palo Alto CA 94303

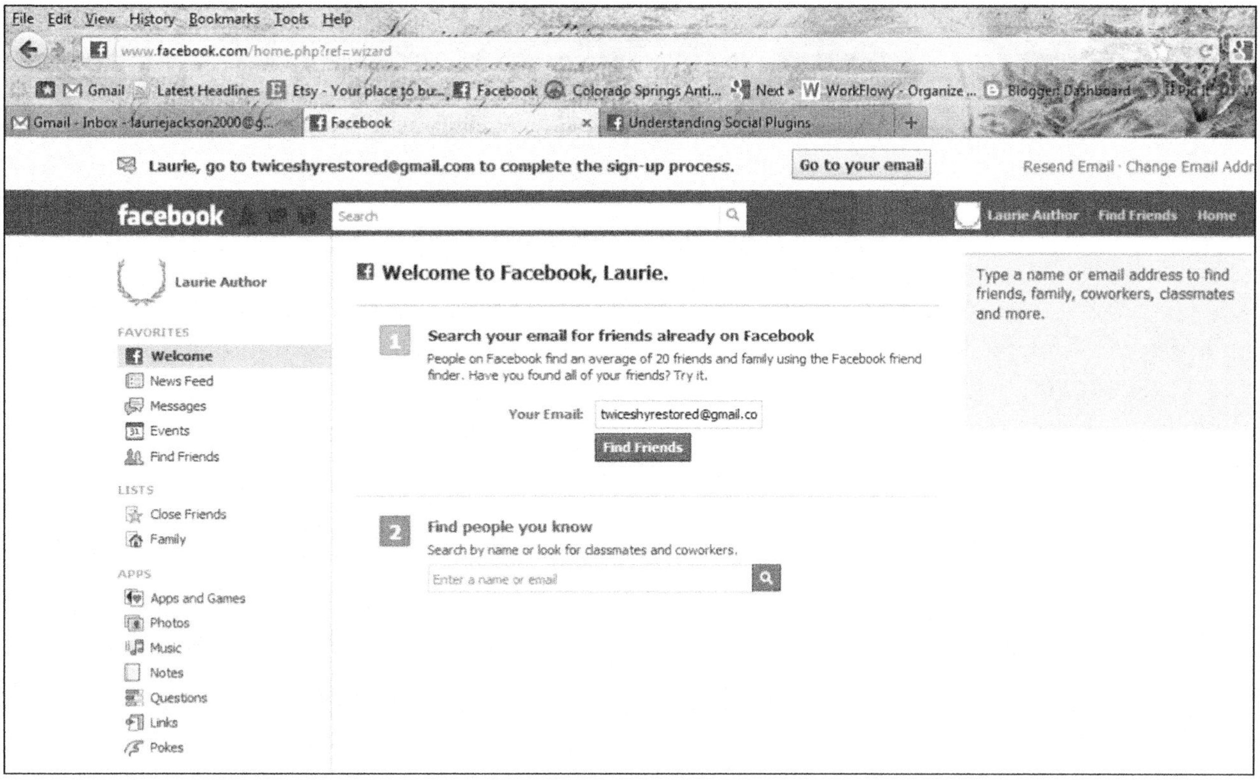
File Edit View History Bookmarks Tools Help
www.facebook.com/home.php?ref=wizard
Facebook
Understanding Social Plugins
Laurie, go to twiceshyrestored@gmail.com to complete the sign-up process.
Go to your email
Resend Email · Change Email Addr
facebook
Laurie Author
Find Friends
Home
FAVORITES
Welcome
News Feed
Messages
Events
Find Friends
LISTS
Close Friends
Family
APPS
Apps and Games
Photos
Music
Notes
Questions
Links
Pokes
Welcome to Facebook, Laurie.
Search your email for friends already on Facebook
People on Facebook find an average of 20 friends and family using the Facebook friend finder. Have you found all of your friends? Try it.
Your Email:
twiceshyrestored@gmail.co
Find Friends
Find people you know
Search by name or look for classmates and coworkers.
Enter a name or email
Type a name or email address to find friends, family, coworkers, classmates and more.

The getting started page

The purpose of the Getting Started page is to find people you know who are already using Facebook. You can enter your email address book and let Facebook tell you which of your contacts are on Facebook. You can also look up friends individually by entering their name in a Search field. You can skip this step if you like.

View and Edit Your Profile.

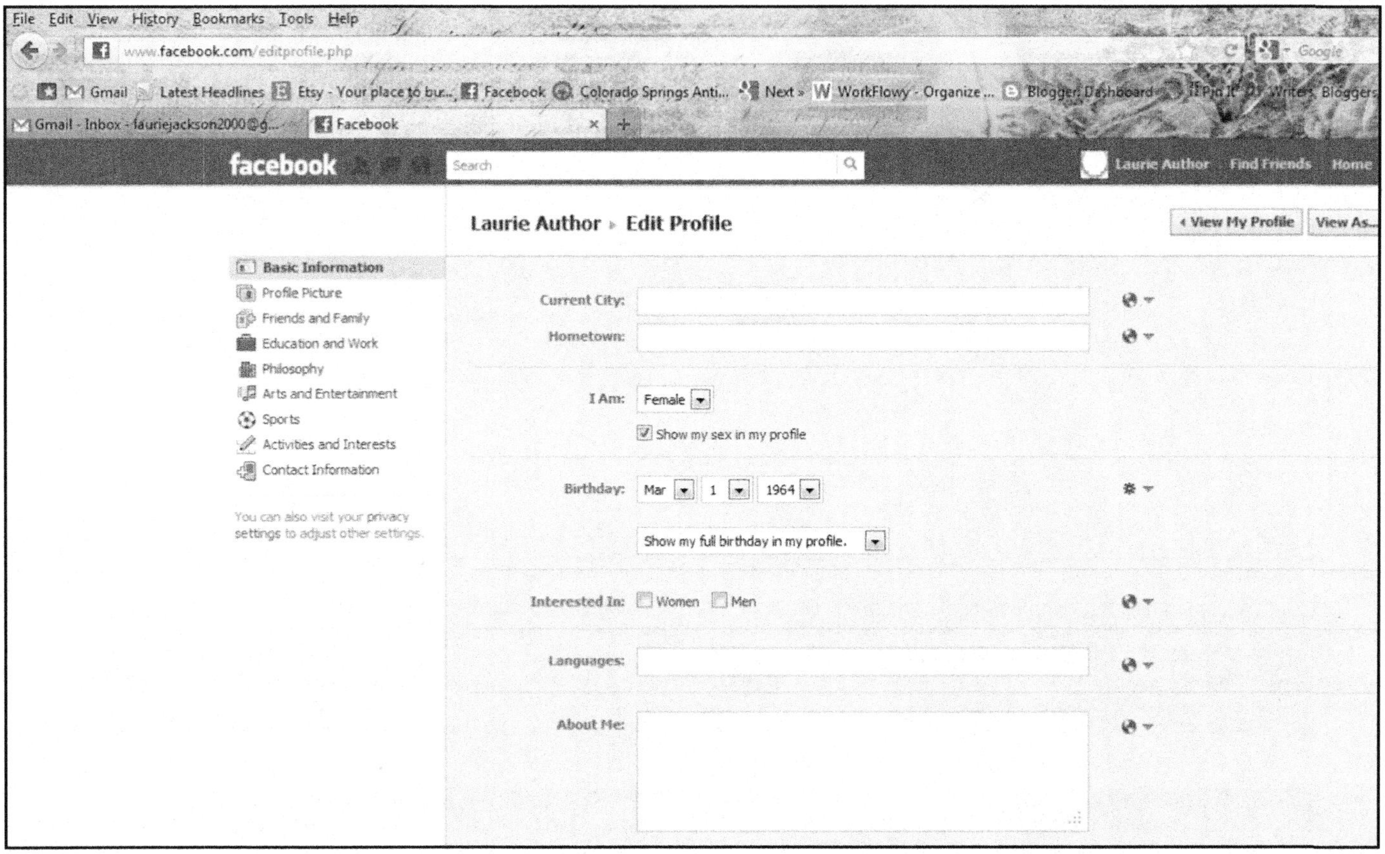

This is your chance to tell the world as much (or as little) about yourself as you choose. At the top of the screen you can click on a box called Edit Profile. Here are some of the kinds of information you might choose to let people see:

- Current City
- Hometown
- Sex
- Birthday
- Whether you are interested in women or men
- Languages spoken
- About me–a place to type in any other written information you would like to be included in your profile

If you're using Facebook mainly to promote yourself or your business, you should give some thought to what kinds of information you want to include in your personal profile. For example, there is no reason to alienate potential customers or employers by informing the world that you belong to a particular political or religious group—unless your purpose is to network with folks belonging to that group. If you decide later to remove some information from your profile, just click **Edit Information** and delete whatever you like.

Add a Profile Picture. Facebook is all about faces. Your profile picture becomes an essential part of your online identity. People see your profile picture when they search for you, and your friends see it when they click on your profile. Many people choose a candid shot rather than a posed photo for their profile picture, probably because candid shots are usually more interesting. They give people a better sense of who you are.

Facebook accepts most common types of digital photos. To add a profile picture, click on the silhouette on the top left of your profile page. You will be asked to either upload a photo from your computer or to use your computer's webcam to add a photo. You can change your profile picture at any time by clicking on it and following the directions. Now you can include even more information by clicking "Info" on the left side of the page.

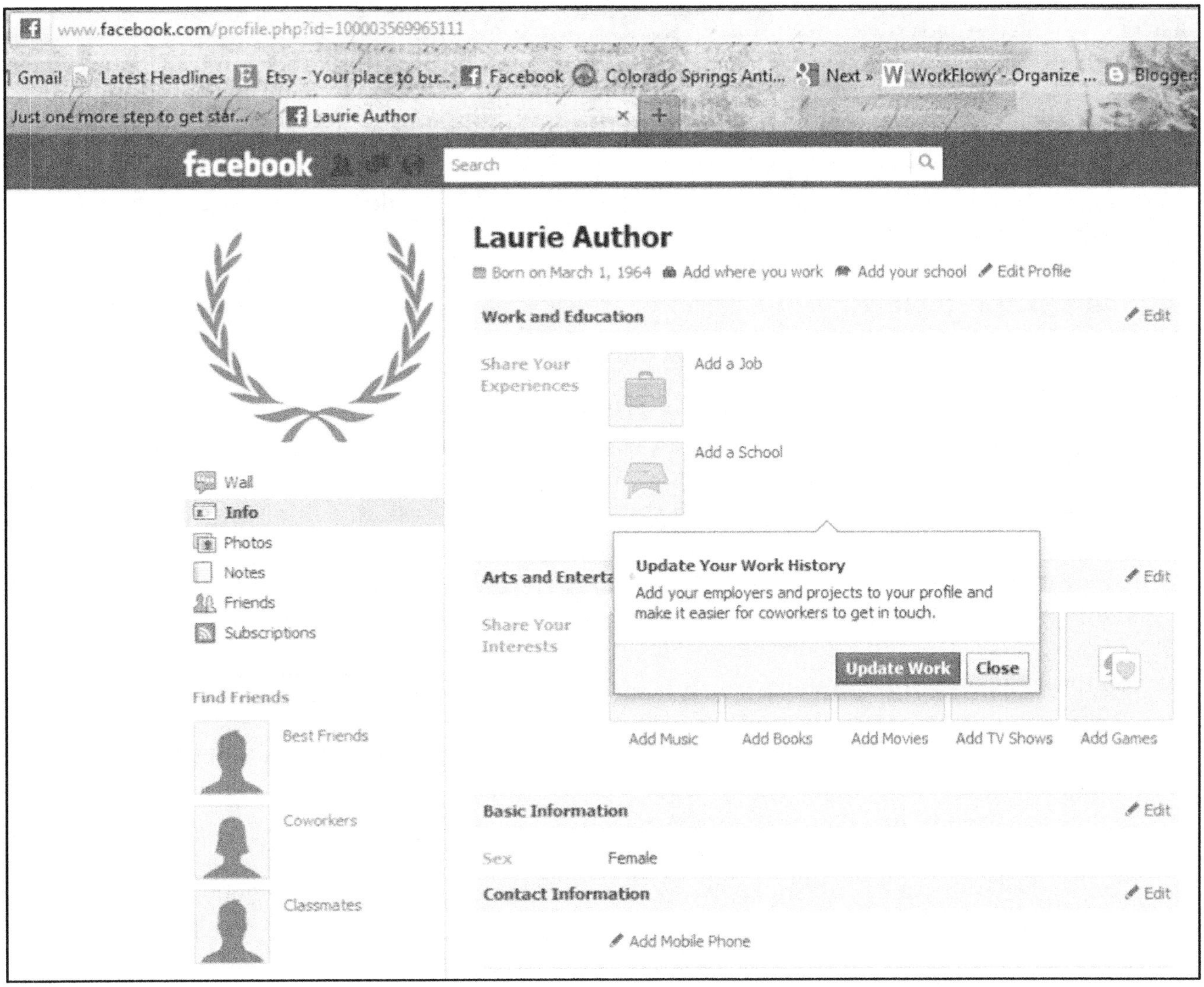

The first section is called Work and Education. Click on the pencil icon and the word Edit next to it and you may then fill in the name of your employer, where you went to college, and where you went to high school. Facebook likes everyone to add this basic information to their accounts, and you will notice that unless/until you do, you will see a prompt at the top of your page asking you to add it!

The second section is called Arts and Entertainment. Here you may click on the different icons to enter information about music, books, movies, TV shows, and games.

The third section is called Basic Information. Here is where the personal information you already entered under Profile will show up.

Finally there is a section called Contact Information, where you may provide additional phone numbers, instant messaging screen names, your physical address, and the addresses of other places you can be found on the web.

Facebook Pages

Facebook Pages are profiles of your business. They're easy to create and they're free. Just click Create a Page at the bottom of any Facebook screen. You will be guided through the process of setting up your page.

1. **Select a category and name for your page.** The name should be the exact name of your product or business. Choose one of the categories listed. If you don't see a category that fits your business precisely, pick the closest match.

2. **Add a profile picture.** Choose a picture that will look good even when it is shown as a thumbnail.

3. **Add information.** Tell people all about your product or service. The more information you add, the better. Think about the questions that your potential customers are likely to have. What do they care about? What's important to them? Tell people everything they need to know to make it as easy as possible for them to do business with you.

4. **Make it captivating.** What keeps you on a given page for any length of time? It all comes down to interesting content. Add as many engaging photos as you can find. Use video if you have it. One of your goals is to build a community of loyal customers. Every aspect of your page should reinforce the idea of community.

5. **Publish your page.** Tell all your friends and customers about your page. Remember that connections on Facebook are exponential, or what some people call "viral." Each of your Facebook friends has friends, and those people have friends, and on and on.

6. **Keep your page current.** Add news, comments and announcements frequently. Using new photos is an easy and effective way to freshen up your page.

We'll delve much deeper into Facebook Pages later.

Facebook Ads

Advertising has become so pervasive that it's nearly lost its effectiveness. The more often people are bombarded with ads, the more they tend to tune out the messages. The most effective ads put information about a product or a service right in front of you at just the right time, almost as if marketers were reading your mind. That is the basic strategy behind Google's advertising. When you perform a search, Google shows you ads directly related to the topic you're looking for. Google's email program, Gmail, searches your incoming messages and shows you ads related to key words in the text.

With Facebook, you can target your ads precisely by age, gender, location and many other variables. When you create your ad, you can decide if you want it to direct people to your own website, to a Facebook page, or to some other location on Facebook, such as a Groups or Events page.

The unique thing about Facebook ads is their "social action." When someone is shown your ad, Facebook shows them how many of their friends have interacted with your Page. For example, your ad might say, "Visit our restaurant today! Your friend Betty Blue Likes it."

You will receive regular reports on your ads' performance (how many people have seen it, how many have clicked on it, etc.). You will also receive useful demographic information to help you ensure that you are reaching the right audience.

We'll explore Facebook's paid advertising in Chapters 10 and 11.

Facebook Platform

Facebook Platform requires some technical knowhow, but it might be a valuable tool for you. One of the most popular applications developed for Facebook Platform is "iLike," a music sharing website. Each month, over six million Facebook users connect with iLike to add music to their profiles. If you have an online application like this that you think Facebook members could use or enjoy, check out Facebook Platform.

Facebook offers some unique and exciting ways to connect with customers. But before you can do that, you will probably want to create an account. To learn how, go on to the next chapter.

2 ► THE FACEBOOK HOME PAGE

It's easy to find your way around Facebook, but the terminology can be a little confusing at first. Consider this chapter a guided tour.

The Facebook homepage is the page you see when you click on Home in the upper right corner of any Facebook page. It is not to be confused with your profile page, which is the page that shows your Newsfeed. To switch to your profile page, click on your name where it appears at the top of your page next to your profile photo.

Blue menu bar

The dark blue menu bar appears at the top of every Facebook page. You can click on any of these options next to the word Facebook:

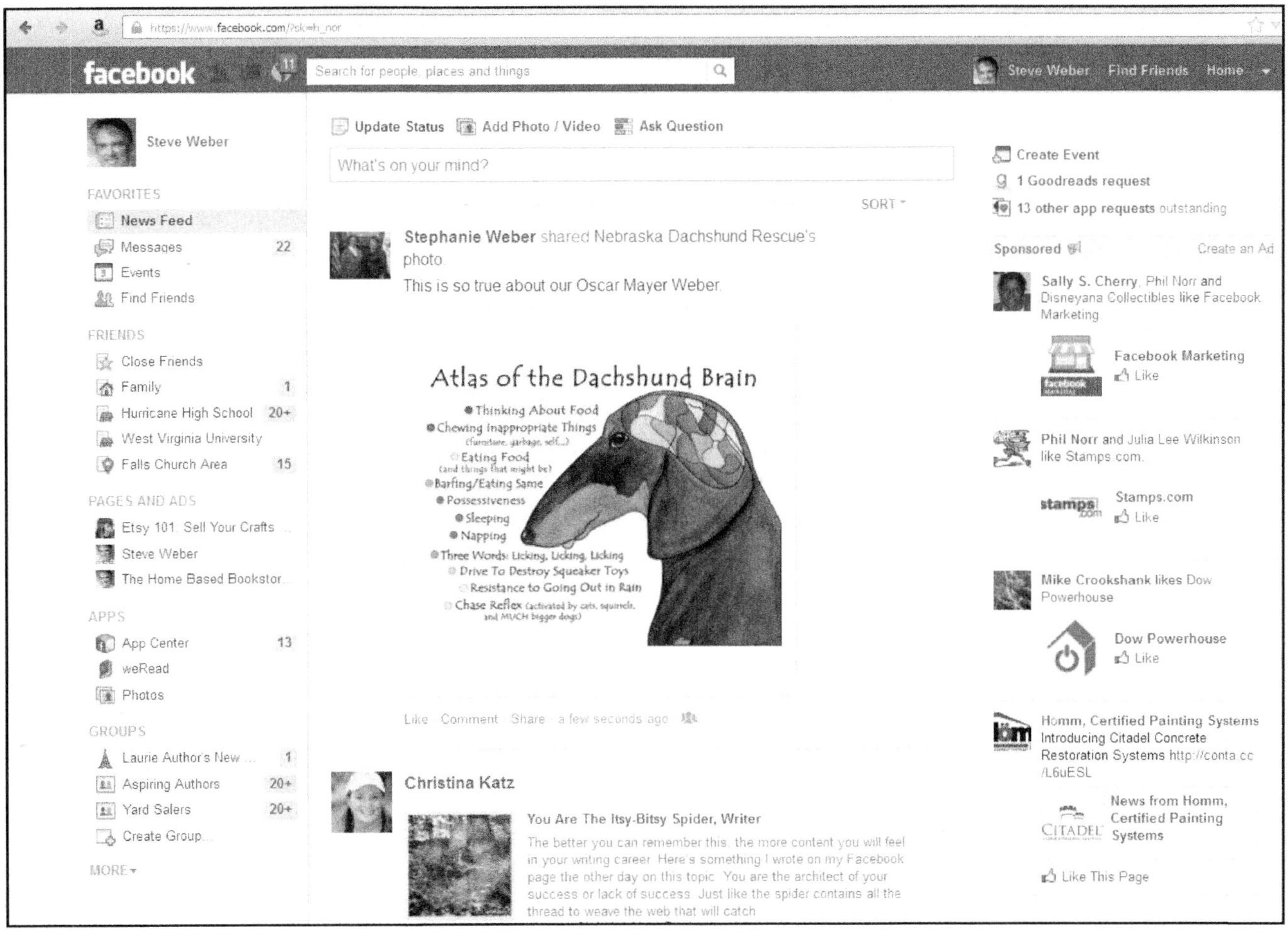

Friends icon

This icon is a silhouette of two people. When you click on the Friends icon, a pull-down menu will appear listing, on the left, Friend Requests and giving you a status of either "No new requests" or a red number indicating that you have that number of requests. On the right you can click on "Find Friends" and you will go to a menu to help you search for Friends. On the bottom of the menu you can click on "See All Friends" for a list of your Friends.

Messages icon

A number next to the Messages icon will tell you how many new messages you have. If there is no number, you have no new messages. Anyone on Facebook can send you a message (unless you change your privacy settings). When you click on the icon, a pull-down menu will appear; click on Messages to read and reply to messages you have received, or to view previous messages. Click on Send a New Message on the right of the screen and a box will appear; enter a friend's name or email address, and then the message. You may click on the paper clip icon to attach a file to your message, or click on the camera icon to attach a photo. You may also choose to click on a mobile phone icon if you wish the message to be forwarded to a mobile address.

On the bottom of the menu you can click on "See All Messages." You have the option to:

- Set up email notifications,
- Turn on text messaging,
- Enable chatting on your page, or;
- Set up video calling.

At the right of this screen, you may also click on the box "+ New Message" to send a message; you may also click on the Search icon to search your archived messages.

Globe icon

A number next to the Globe icon will tell you how many new notifications you have. If there is no number, you have no new notifications. You will receive notifications about activities that your friends are doing that might be of interest to you. For example, if a friend comments on your status or a friend posts in a group that you belong to, you might receive a notification. When you click on the Globe icon, there is a pull-down menu called Notifications and below it you will see them, or the message "No New Notifications." At the bottom of the menu you may click on "See All Notifications." On the page that comes up you may choose to receive notifications via Text Message or RSS feed. You may also click on the words at the right of the screen, "Notification Settings," to decide when you would like Facebook to send you an email. You may choose never to be notified, or to be notified whenever anything involving you happens on Facebook, such as when someone mentions you in a comment, tags you in a photo, or makes a change in a group you belong to.

Search

A handy white search box appears in the middle of the Facebook menu bar; you need only type in a search query and click on the magnifying glass.

Profile

This option takes you to the profile you created when you joined Facebook. You can edit anything on your profile and add or remove information.

Find Friends

From here you can manage your Friend list and locate, add and invite Friends.

Home

Wherever you wander in Facebook, click on home to return to your home page.

Down-facing arrow

Click here to change the settings for your account and your privacy protection. You can also Log Out of your account here (which you will want to do if you're using a public computer), and reach the Help menu.

On the Left: Filters

The column on the left of your home page is a list of "filters" that allow you to select what you would like to see in the center of your home page. Those filters are divided into sections: Favorites, Pages, Groups, Apps and Friends. The default view is one of the choices under Favorites, and "Welcome" will appear until you have added some Friends. After that, "News Feed" becomes the default setting that is selected automatically when you log in to Facebook. News Feed displays posts from all your friends on the center of your screen. It lets you keep up, in real time, with what your friends are doing.

Other filters in this column allow you to change what you would like to see displayed on the center of your screen. For example, you can view applications you have already added to your account, events you have RSVP'd to, and photos you have uploaded.

Let's explore the filter, "Friends."

When adding Friends, Facebook gives you the option to label them into the Close Friends, Acquaintances and Restricted Lists. Listing people this way affects the frequency that their status updates will appear in your News Feed: Close Friends show up more than Acquaintances, and those on the Restricted list can only see posts and profile info you make public. Facebook uses something called Smart Lists to automatically create sublists of your friends as coworkers, classmates, local friends and family members based on your friends' profile information and the information you have already provided in your own profile. When you Friend someone who works at the same company you did, as listed in both of your profiles, Facebook automatically categorizes them into your Work Friends list. It also does this with School Friends, Local Friends, and Family.

You can create your own customized filter by hovering over the word "Friends" in the column, and then clicking on the word "More" when it appears to the right of the column. Suppose you wanted a quick way to keep up with friends in your bowling league. You would click "More," then click on the box that says "+Create List," then give the list a name (such as "bowling"), and then add individual names of your

Facebook Friends. Then Bowling appears as a choice under Friends, and when you click on the Bowling filter, only posts just from everyone in your league will appear on the center of your screen.

In the middle: Wall

The middle of the home page displays whatever you choose in the left column. The default display is News Feed. When you first go to your home page, you will see the latest posts from your friends.

At the top of this part of the home page, there is a box where you may "Update Status" or "Add Photo/Video." Inside the box is the writing prompt, "What's on your mind?"

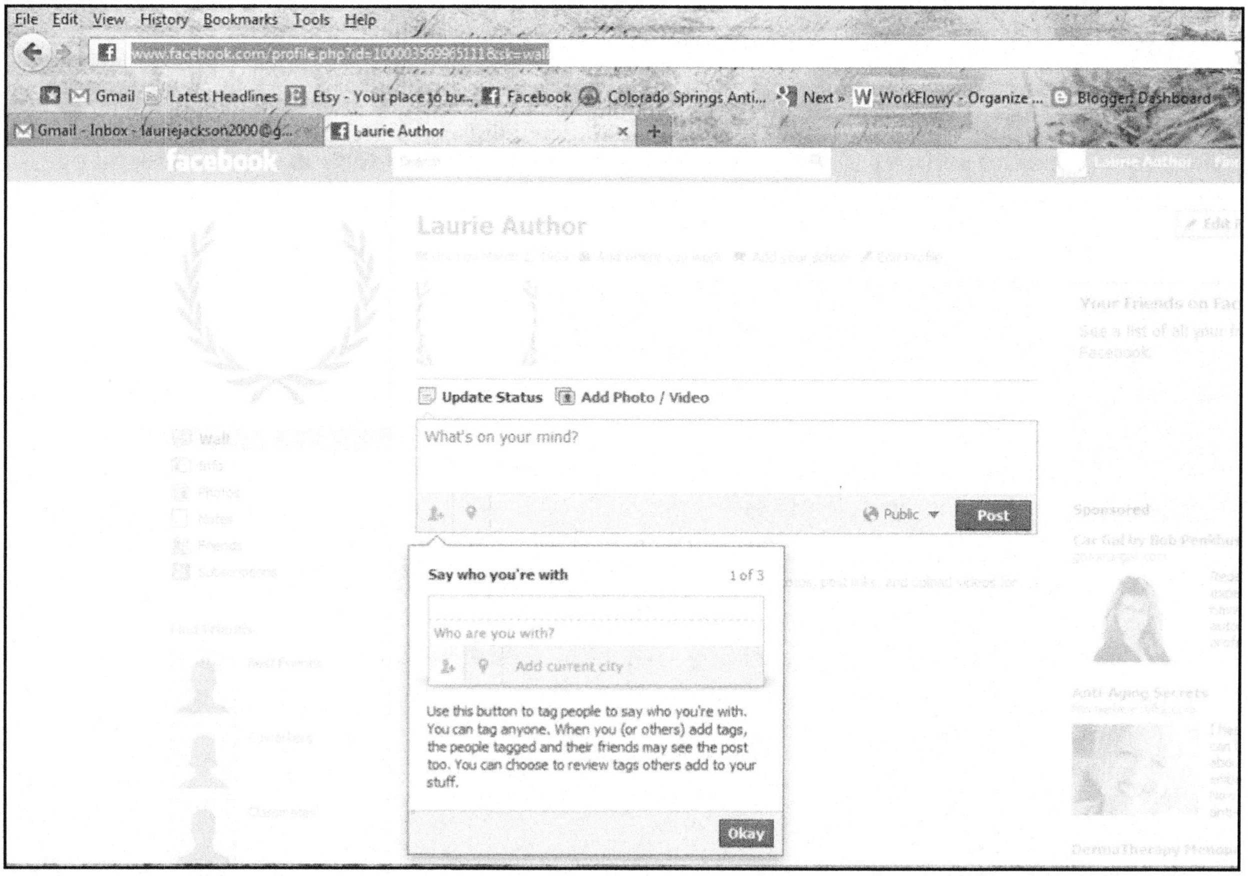

Type anything that you would like all your friends to see in the box and click on the following options below the box:

- **Friends icon**

  The Friends icon is a silhouette with a "+" sign next to it. When you click on this, you will be prompted to type in the name of any of your Facebook friends who are with you. This "tags" them so that the status update will also appear on their Facebook wall.

- **Map pin icon**

  An upside down teardrop shape with a hole in it is the recognized symbol of your location. If you type in a location that Facebook recognizes, it will "tag" that location. Only people who can see your status update can see your location; for example, if you are visiting a popular restaurant that has a

Facebook page and you tag that location, your visit will show up on that restaurant's page only if your privacy settings are set to Public for that status update—and even then, it will only show up to people who have Administrator privileges for that restaurant's page.

- **Globe icon**

  This is how you set the privacy level for your status update: it defaults to whatever you have your page set at, but you can change the privacy for every individual status update if you wish; here is where you may indicate that you want the status update visible according to those lists/filters you have already set up.

When you are finished, click on the blue box that says "Post." Your status update will then appear on your Wall.

You can also use this box to share photos, videos or Internet links with friends. To add a photo or video, click on Add Photo/Video. To add a link, simply type or paste it into the box and when you click on "post," the link will become a hyperlink. Whatever you post in this box shows up both in your profile and on your friends' home pages, depending upon which privacy settings you have selected.

On the right: highlights

The right column of the home page contains miscellaneous information and ads. At the top of the column you might see requests and invitations from friends or reminders of upcoming birthdays and other events. Below that you will probably see suggestions from Facebook about people you might want to add as friends. These people are typically friends of your friends or members of networks where you belong.

You will probably see sponsored ads in this section of your home page. You might also see an invitation to Like a business that has a Facebook page (more on that later).

At the very bottom of the highlights column you will see the word "English." You can click on this and change languages if you wish. Among the choices for the English language are "English – Pirate", "English – UK", "English – Upside Down", and "English – US." You may also click on "Privacy" to learn about your privacy and Facebook, or "Terms" to review Facebook's terms of service. If you click on "More," you see a list of other links to click on: About, Advertising, Careers, Create a Page, Developers and Help.

On the bottom: navigation tools and help

At the bottom left you will again see the word "English" in case you'd like to use that link to change languages. At the bottom right of the screen you will see the same list of options as when you click on the "More" link mentioned above. Farthest on the right you will find the all-important Help function. Facebook does a good job of keeping its help files up to date. If you don't know how to do something on Facebook or you're just plain stuck, you know where to look.

Now that you know your way around the home page, you can start putting Facebook to work.

3 ▶ FINDING FRIENDS AND KEEPING CONNECTIONS

Facebook uses the word "friends" in a loose sense. Your Facebook friends can be relatives, acquaintances, co-workers or anyone else you would like to keep in touch with. Searching for friends is simple. Click on "Find Friends" in the blue menu at the top of any Facebook page. You will be given these options to find people:

- **People you email or communicate with:** Facebook has already populated the page with possibilities that you can click on, beginning with whatever email program you used to sign up for your Facebook account. Enter your email address and click "Find Friends." Facebook will search your email account for possible friends. Facebook does not store your password or contact anyone without your permission.
- **Suggestions:** Facebook suggests people you might want to add as friends. These people are usually friends of your current friends on Facebook.
- **Find people via instant messaging (IM) or Skype:** You can import your buddy list from AOL Instant Messenger, Skype or your list of Windows Live contacts.

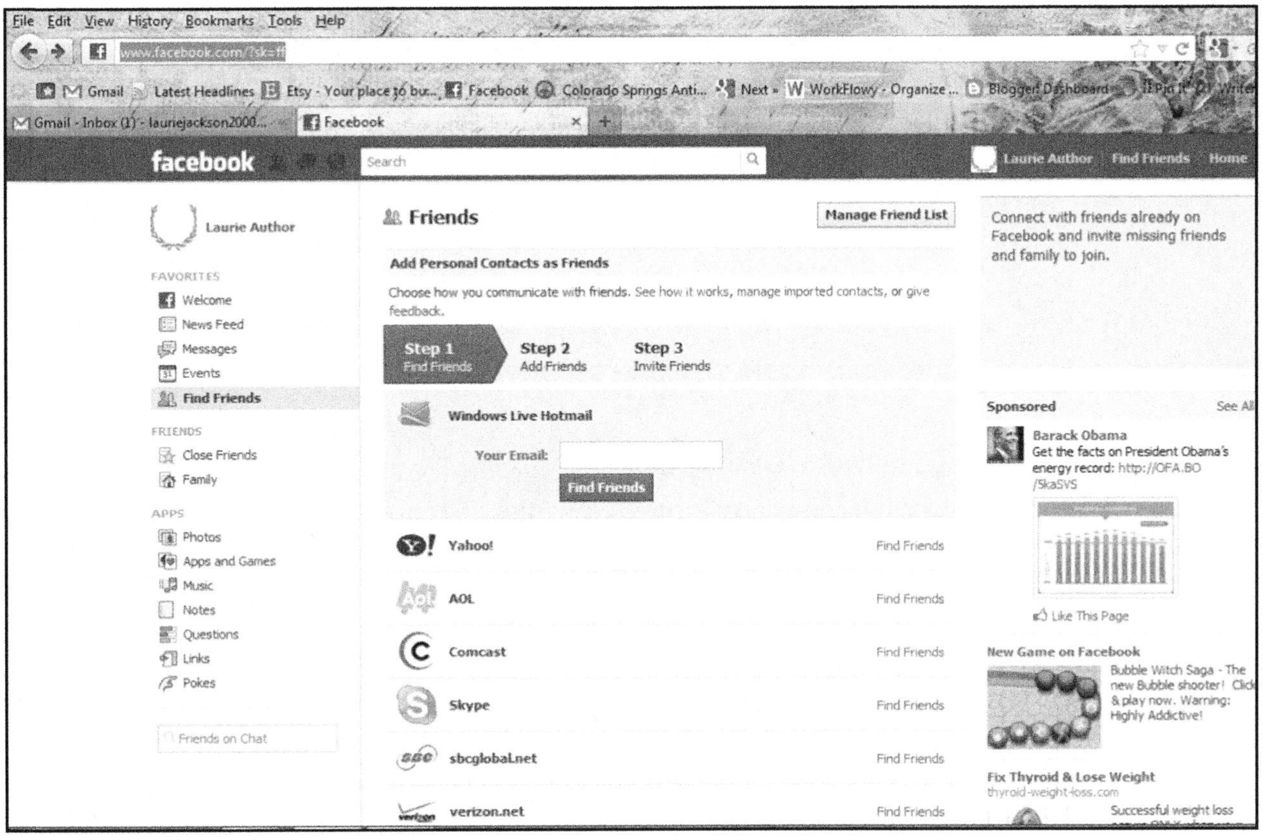

- **Other Tools:** At the bottom of the list of services is an option called Other Tools. Click on that to open a box that will enable you to upload your existing contact file from a service such as Microsoft Outlook, Outlook Express, Windows Contacts, Apple Mail, and others.

Invite a friend by email

You can also use a handy form right on Facebook to send a personal invitation to your friends who aren't already on Facebook. All you need is their email addresses. Facebook will automatically send up to two reminders after the first invite.

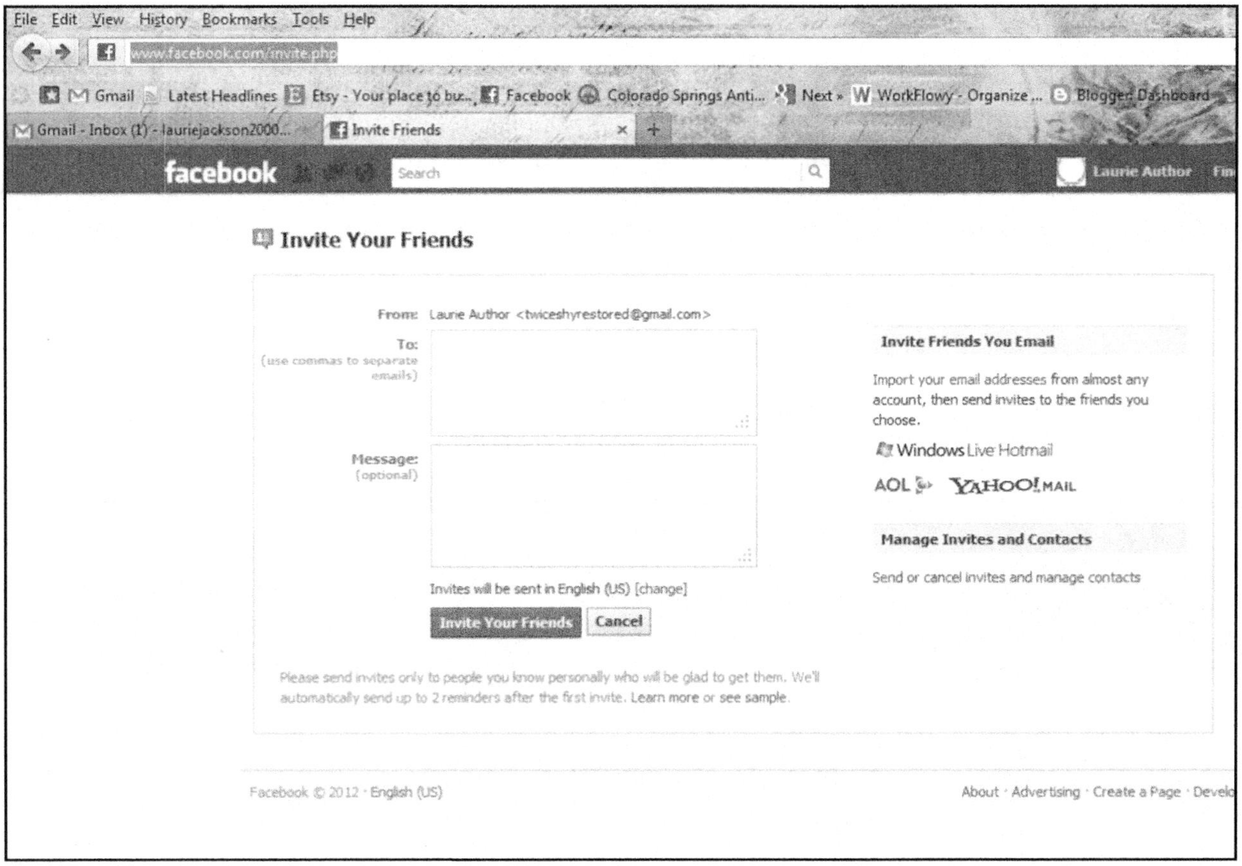

Find Friends, Classmates and Coworkers

This option allows you to search by your hometown, current city, schools you've attended, or employers.

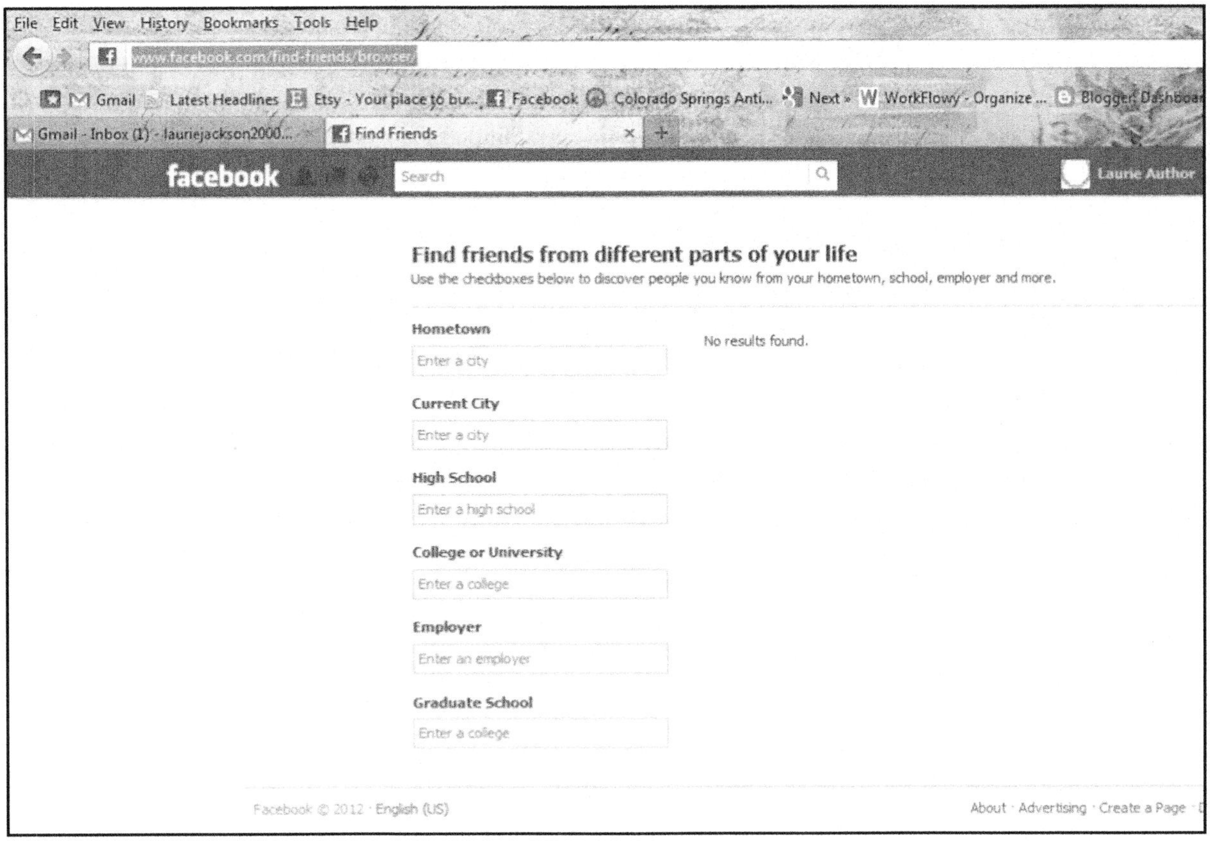

Search for people

You can also just enter the name or email address of someone you would like to find in the Search box at the top of the Facebook page and ask Facebook to look for the person.

Once you have found a potential friend, you can send a friend request to that person. Both parties must agree before the friendship can become active.

Communicating privately

You have a few ways of communicating with friends on Facebook. If you would like your communications to be private, use the "Messages" feature on the blue menu bar at the top of any Facebook page. This feature works much like standard email; you can attach a file or a link to any site on the Internet. You can also forward messages you have received to anyone, as long as you know their email address, by clicking on the box marked Actions at the top right of the screen and choosing the option Forward.

You can send a message to anyone on Facebook even if the person is not a friend. Likewise, anyone on Facebook can send you a message. If you would like to restrict who can send you a message, select "Privacy Settings" by clicking on the arrow at the far right of the blue menu bar. Go to the "How You Connect" section of the Privacy page and click on Edit Settings. This gives you the option to limit who can look you up using your email address or phone number, who can send you friend requests, and who can send you Facebook messages.

When you send someone a message, a notification appears in the person's email inbox. A notification also appears next to "Messages" on the blue menu at the top of the person's home page on Facebook. You can also initiate the message feature when you are viewing a friend's profile by clicking the box at the far right of your screen that says "Messages."

Going public: Writing on a friend's Wall

If you would like the world to see your message, you can write on a friend's wall. The wall is the center of a person's Facebook profile. (The next chapter has more about profiles.)

Your wall appears in the center of your profile page. You can use your wall to post anything about yourself that you would like your friends to see. Your friends can write on your wall and you can write on theirs. To write on a friend's wall, visit their profile by clicking on their photo icon on the left side of your wall. This will take you to their profile page. Then you can type something in the "What's on your mind?" box at the top of the wall and click "Post."

4 ► BUILDING YOUR PROFILE

When you first set up your account, you entered some basic information about yourself—your birth date, sex and regional network. You might have also added information about your education and employment. You might even have filled in the blanks for things like religion, political affiliation, activities, interests and favorite things.

All this information becomes part of your Facebook profile—the public face that you present to the world when they click on your name from any Facebook page. If you want to use Facebook for promotional as well as personal reasons, you need to give some careful thought to the image you want to project. Here are a few suggestions:

- **Keep it real.** Drop the slogans and anything else that sounds like it belongs in a TV commercial. Facebook users are turned off by hype and phoniness. Give people real information about yourself and your organization.

- **Keep it current**. Yes, it takes some time to keep your information up to date, but news is the lifeblood of Facebook and any social networking site. People keep coming back to profiles that have new and relevant information.

- **Keep it interesting.** Share information that will appeal to other people. Do you love kayaking or bird watching or bowling? Those interests might not have anything to do with what you are trying to promote, but they create a picture of you. They give people a sense of who you are and what makes you interesting.

Choosing who sees what

Facebook allows you to customize who has access to specific types of information about you. Here's how:

- Choose "Privacy Settings" under the arrow at the far right of the blue menu bar.
- Choose "Profile and Tagging" and then click on Edit Settings.

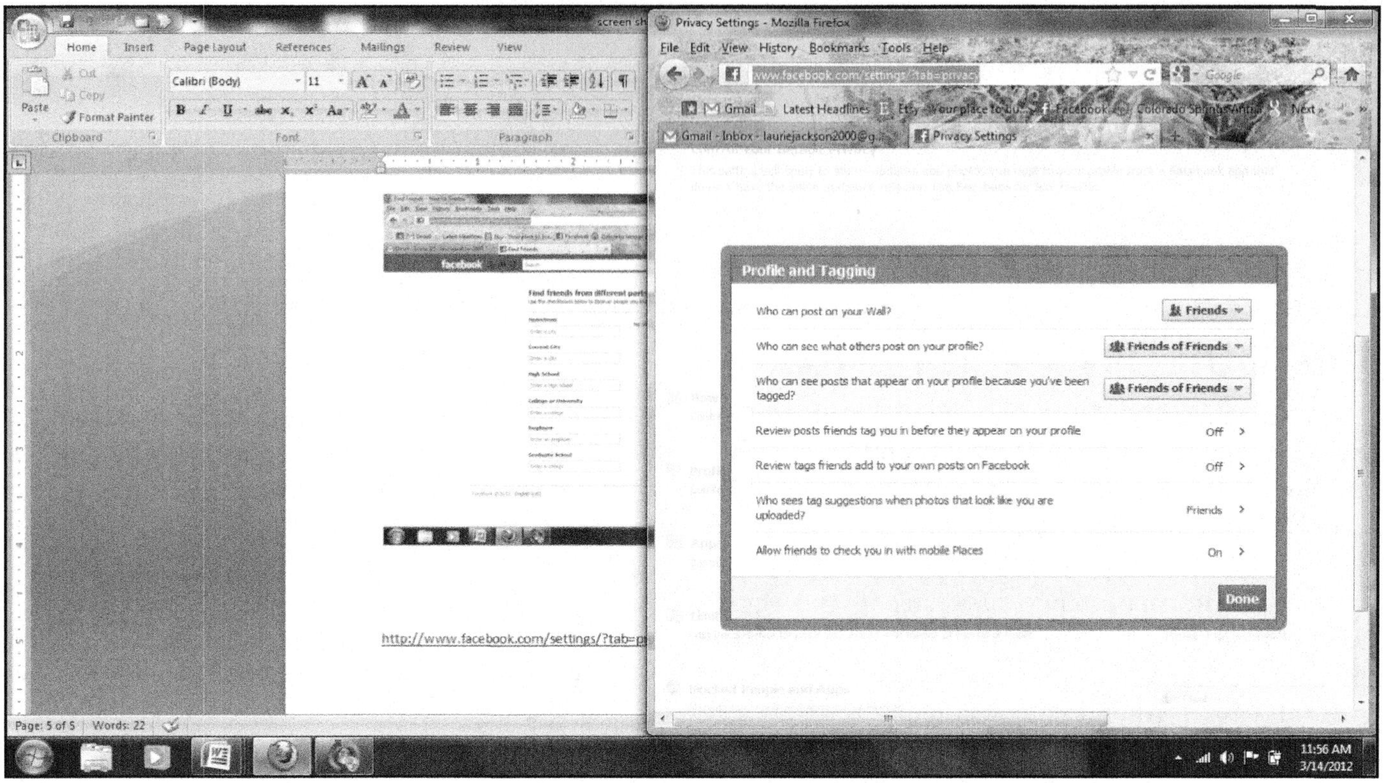

- Choose who will have access to specific types of information.

Control your default privacy

This applies to status updates and photos you post to your profile from a Facebook app that doesn't have the inline audience selector.

For each type of information, you can decide if you will allow it to be seen by:

- Everyone
- Friends of friends
- Your networks and friends
- Customized lists
- Any of the filters you have already designated, such as Close Friends, Family, etc.

The last two options allow you to choose which networks will be given access to specific types of information. You can also keep specific individuals from seeing specific types of information.

The privacy settings allow you to control who may:

- Post on your wall
- See what others post on your profile
- See posts that appear on you profile because you've been tagged

You also have three "On/Off" switches you can set to designate if you would like to review posts friends tag you in before they appear on your profile, or tags they add to your posts on Facebook, or whether friends are allowed to check you in with Mobile Places. You can also designate who can see tags that are suggested by Facebook when photos are uploaded, as Facebook uses face recognition technology to identify users whenever a photo is uploaded by anyone.

Facebook is able to remain free to use because Facebook users are the product being sold–sold to advertisers. It seems a fair trade for all the fun and opportunity available to you as a Facebook user. To protect your privacy, it is important to pay attention to your privacy setting. Facebook works hard to inform you whenever you are in a position to have your data accessed by any friend, network, or application. You should be diligent to take advantage of these opportunities to protect your privacy.

Facebook takes appropriate precautions to protect user information by using secure pages–but never forget that whenever you're using the Internet, you are in a public place. Just as there will be thieves waiting for an opportunity to enter your home while you're away and steal your belongings, there are people who troll the Internet looking for a way to access your personal information. Be aware.

The best way to keep your Facebook account secure is to:

- Use the privacy settings
- Like the Facebook Site Governance page to keep up to date with any Privacy Policy changes
- Use a password that is unique to Facebook

Be informed about what Facebook is doing with your information. Visit the Facebook Data Use Policy page on Facebook: http://www.facebook.com/about/privacy/#basicinfo. (Remember, when you signed up for Facebook you agreed to their terms, and that you have read and understand the Data Use Policy!)

5 ► SHARING PHOTOS

Facebook is the most heavily used photo-sharing site on the web. It is probably not the best; others offer more features. What sets Facebook apart is the power it gives you to associate photos with particular friends or particular events in your life.

The thing to remember about posting your photos on Facebook, or anywhere else online for that matter, is that they will remain accessible on Facebook's servers indefinitely—even if you delete them. Exercise discretion and especially if you are using Facebook for promotional purposes for your business or other endeavor, do not post any photos that you wouldn't want your grandmother or your best customer or prospective client to see.

Uploading photos

Facebook makes it easy to organize your photos by allowing you to create separate albums for particular events or particular groups of friends. For example, you might decide to create an album for photos of your most recent vacation or your college reunion. Or you might create a family album or an album of your bridesmaids. An album can include up to 200 photos. If you have more than that, just start a new album.

To upload photos, Add Photo/Video at the top of your page. Then click on Create Photo Album.

Click on **Select Photos to Upload**. You will see a directory of all the folders on your hard drive. Navigate to the folders where you have stored your photos. Select the photos you want to use and click Upload. You now have a photo album!

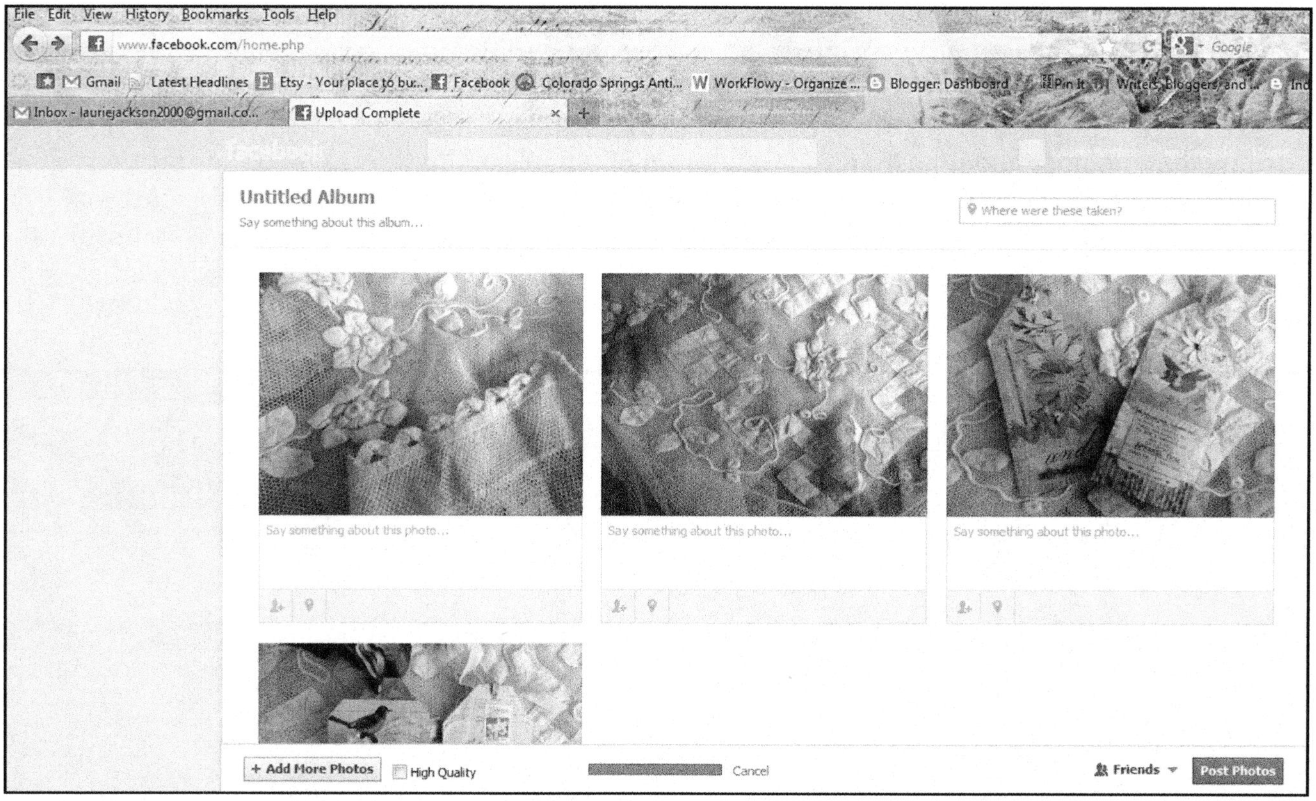

Once you have selected photos and they have uploaded, you will be asked to provide information about the photos:

- **Album Name:** In the upper left corner of the screen, you will see a box and the words, Untitled Album. You can type over those words in the box with the name you would like to give to the album. For example, Graduation Photos. Beneath the Album Name you can write something about the album (a description, date, etc.)
- **Location:** In the upper right corner of the screen you will see a box with the little map icon, and the words, Where were these taken? Here is where you may identify the location of the photos.
- **Description:** Beneath each photo there is a blank box with the words "Say something about this photo." You may fill in the box with anything you want to say, and whatever you write will appear with the photo on your wall.

- **Tagging:** The shaded blue line beneath the photo's description box has the Friends icon which you can click on to tag Facebook users. Next to it is the Location icon which you can use to specify a location for that particular photo. At the bottom of this screen you have a few more options; you can Add More Photos to this album, or check the High Quality box which will store larger images of your photos (but they will load more slowly).
- **Who can see this?** In the right bottom corner of the screen you can restrict who sees your album by choosing: Public, Friends, Only Me, or Custom. If you choose Custom, you can limit access to particular networks or exclude certain people from seeing your album.

When you have completed this information, click Post Photos.

Editing and tagging Photos

Once you have created your album, you will see a window with all of the photos in the album. You can organize your album from this screen by clicking and dragging to move the photos around. Or you can click on the pencil icon next to the words Edit Album to:

- **Edit photos:** You can use this to add captions, tag certain people in the photos, choose a cover for the album, and move a photo into a different album. (The album cover is the image that will be associated with your album. By default, the first photo in your album becomes the cover, unless you choose a different one.)

When you hover over each photo, two icons will appear: a blank box with the words, Click on a face to tag, and a down-pointing arrow. When you click on the arrow, you will see three more options: Move to other album, Make Album Cover, and Remove this photo.

- **Add Photos:** Choose this to return to the upload function to add more photos to the album.
- **Delete Photos:** Clicking on the garbage can icon will delete the entire album.

When you have finished editing your photos, click the blue box marked Done.

Viewing photos of yourself

If you would like to see all the photos and videos in which you have been tagged, click Photos under your profile picture. If you don't see a box on that page called "Photos and Videos of You," that means no one has tagged you in their photos.

If you don't want to be tagged in a photo, you can remove the tag that identifies you. If you don't want the photo to appear at all, you will have to contact the person who is displaying it on their page and ask them to remove it.

6 ► JOINING OR STARTING A GROUP

Facebook Groups are online communities of Facebook users who share a common interest. Groups are different from Pages, which you can follow on Facebook by simply clicking on Like. Groups are communities that you actually join if they are open. There are groups for just about anything you can imagine. For example:

- Younger legs for older runners: Advice for older athletes.
- When I was your age, Pluto was a planet: Off-beat science discussions.
- Join to support breast cancer awareness month: An advocacy group.

Groups are basically meeting places where people who have a common interest can hold discussions and share news, photos, videos and links. When you join a group, the other members do not have access to your profile. Your normal privacy restrictions apply.

Groups offer some interesting marketing possibilities. Let's look at an example. Suppose you have written a book about Agatha Christie. You could join one (or more) of the 99 Facebook groups devoted to the famous mystery writer. Then when you join a discussion, you might just mention something you discovered in researching your book. This is basically free marketing.

A few words of caution: First, if you contribute to a discussion, your contribution should actually have some relation to the shared interests of the group. For example, don't start talking about your web design services on the discussion board of a group devoted to the Pittsburgh Steelers. The administrator of the group may delete your post, and other members of the group will probably be angry about your irrelevant comments.

Even if your contribution to a discussion is relevant, you don't want it to sound too much like an advertisement. With a little creativity, you should be able to write something that sounds more like an announcement than a commercial.

Joining a group

The first step in joining a group is choosing one from among the thousands of groups available. Just type in a few key words in the search bar at the top of any Facebook page and see what turns up. For example, if you type "Boston Celtics," you will get a list of all the places on Facebook devoted to that legendary basketball team. You can then click on the Search Filter in the left sidebar, Groups. (If you don't narrow the search to Groups, you can tell which are Groups rather than Pages because there will be a bar to the left that says "Join Group" rather than "Like.") The Groups that are open to be joined will say "Open Group" below the name. If it says "Closed Group," you will need to be invited by a member.

Explore a few of the groups that your search turns up to see which ones might be worth joining. You can check out most groups without joining them just by clicking on the name of the group. In particular check out the discussions to see if they are worth reading. If you like what you see and the group is open, just click "Join This Group." You can also be added to a group by a friend who is already a member. And you may be swayed to join the group with the most members.

On the group's home page, you will find:

- Basic information about the group
- A list of members (click on About next to the name of the group at the top of the page)
- A discussion board
- A wall much like your own wall on Facebook
- Photos
- Links

You can use the links function to add a link to another group or to a Facebook page (more about pages in the next chapter). You can use Facebook pages to promote yourself or your business.

Keep in mind that the group's administrator can delete a link for any reason.

Creating a group

If you're unsatisfied with any of the groups on Facebook, or if you just want to add your own personal touch, you can create a group yourself.

Begin by clicking on the arrow next to the word "Home" in upper right corner of your page, then choose "Help," then click on "Visit the Help Center." In the search bar at the top of that page, type in "Create Group." Click on "How do I create a group?" and ignore the instructions you see there; instead, click on "Learn more about groups." You will be taken to a page with a green bar you can press, "Create Group."

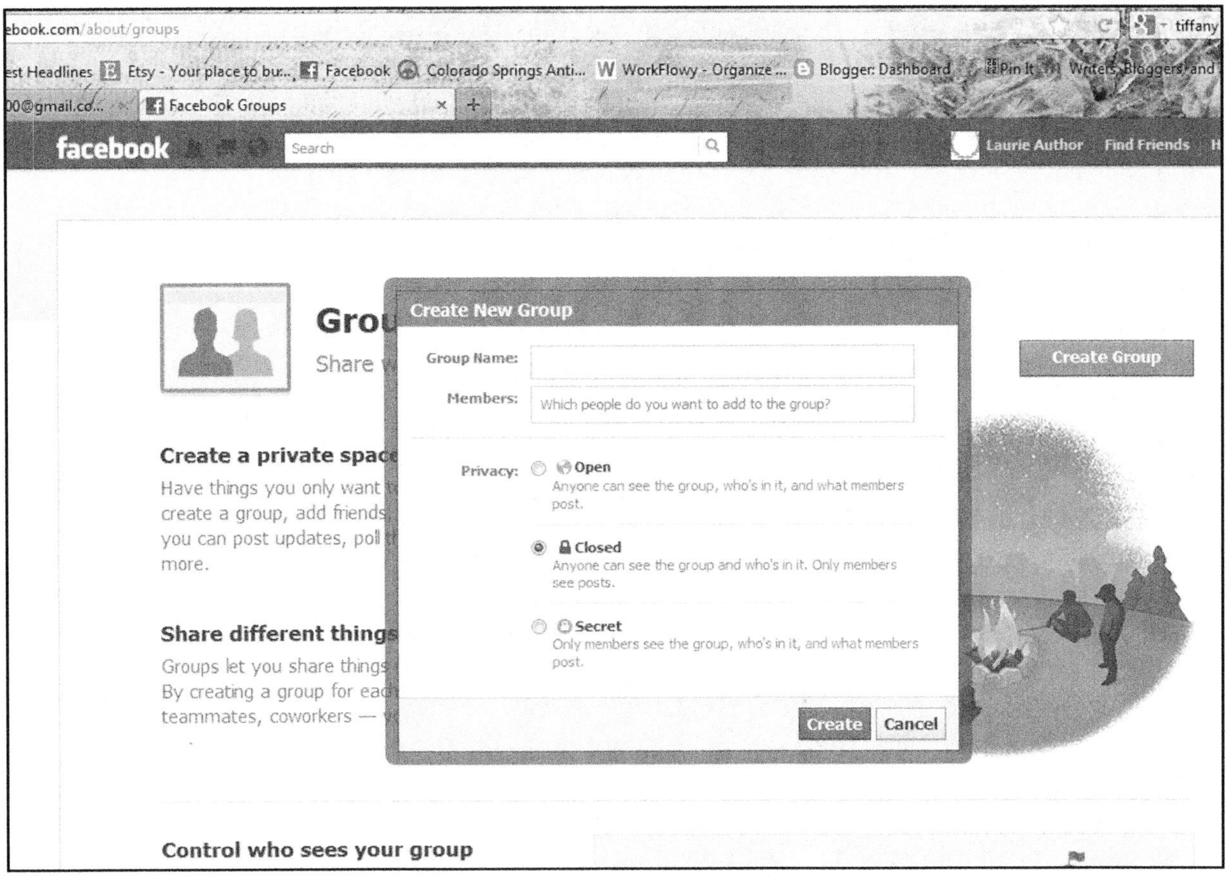

You'll need to provide some basic information about your group including:

- **Name:** Think of something catchy (or at least descriptive).
- **Members:** You will need to indicate which people you want to add to the group.
- **Privacy:** The options are "Open," "Closed" and "Secret." Open means anyone can see the group, who's in it, and what members post. With Closed, anyone can see the group and who's in it, but only members see posts. Only members can see Secret groups, who's in them, and what members post.

When you start a group, you automatically become its administrator. You can then appoint other administrators at your discretion. Administrators have control over the group's content and membership.

When you establish a group, you can invite your Facebook friends to join it. If you decide to make membership open to anyone on Facebook (most groups are), then other people can join if they're interested.

Your group page will appear in the left hand column of your home page, under the heading Groups. When you click on it, you will be taken to the Group's page and from there you can Write a post, Add Photo/Video, Ask Question or Upload File, just like you can on your own personal page. Members may also do these same things.

If you decide that running your group is more trouble than it is worth, you can just delete it. You might have to delete all of its members first, and then leave the group before it is deleted. On the other hand, you might decide that groups offer a fairly easy way of building a community of people who are interested in what you would like to promote.

Once you've created your first group, it is easier to create more, as you will then have a filter on the left of your home page called Groups and an icon to click on that says, Create a Group!

Groups and market research

Besides providing free exposure, groups can also give you valuable information about what people think of particular products or services—either yours or your competitors'. By spending some time on the discussion board in a group, you can get a good sense of what people love or hate about whatever you are trying to promote.

Suppose you have an online business selling quilting supplies. You can drop in on one of the 44 groups devoted to quilting and check out what people are saying about various quilting products. What are people looking for that they are having a hard time finding? How do people feel about buying quilting products online? How can you find the right niche that will allow your business to grow? This type of research might not be scientific, but it can really open your eyes to new business opportunities.

An easy way to do this is by using the Ask Question option at the top of the Group page. Click on Ask Question and you will see a box that says Ask something. Just type in your question, such as, "Where is your favorite source of fabric online?" You can add options you have already thought of, and also give your group members the option of adding their own option/answer. As friends answer the question, their responses appear next to the question.

7 ▶ FACEBOOK PAGES

A Facebook Page is a public profile of your business, brand or organization. You can use a Page to promote your organization, capture new audiences, and share information with your people who have Liked your Page. (Pages have people who Like them, or "users" rather than "friends.") This is part of Facebook's effort to keep Pages completely separate from a user's personal profile.

There are a few important differences between pages and personal profiles. Pages are strictly for "professional" rather than personal use. Your Page and your profile remain separate. Your users will not know that you are the administrator of your page, unless you tell them by posting identifying information on the page, and they won't have access to your personal profile.

Facebook is very serious about keeping personal profiles strictly personal. Features like friending and messaging are intended only for personal uses. For example, if you invite a person to become a friend, that person will become a friend of your personal profile, not your page. If you try to use your personal profile for promotional purposes, Facebook may consider this spamming and may disable your account, sometimes called "The Facebook Slap."

So if you want to use Facebook for promotional purposes without paying for ads, you have two alternatives: groups or pages.

Groups vs. Pages: Which is better?

In the previous chapter we saw that groups are an effective way to create a community of people who have shared interests. Groups focus on discussion rather than promotion. They make it easy for members to share ideas and opinions.

Pages are more like websites. They give you much more control over how you present your organization. Take a look, for example, at the Facebook Page for the Museum of Modern Art in New York (www.facebook.com/pages/New-York-NY/MoMA-The-Museum-of-Modern-Art/).

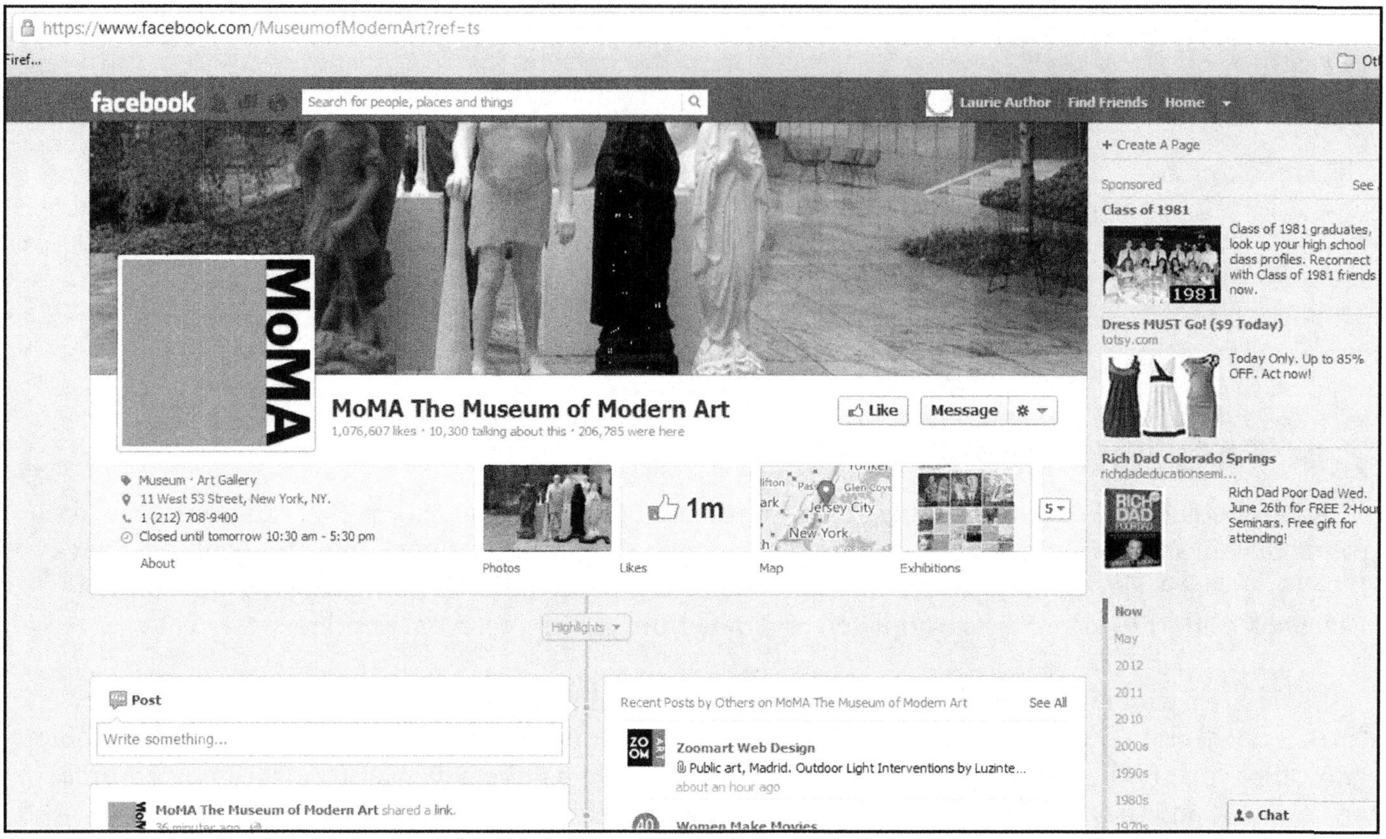

This page has more than a million Likes, and it's easy to see why. The wall section of the page contains brief descriptions and photos of current exhibits and activities, along with comments from visitors. You can also find information about the museum's hours and coming events. You can view selected photos of the museum and watch videos. The message of this page is clear: The museum is an exciting, vibrant place where something new is happening all the time.

Pages typically have a clear message like this that tries to create a favorable impression of an organization. Groups, on the other hand, are more like discussion forums. Their focus is more on the views of members than the message you would like to communicate. Still, groups offer an appealing channel for the kind of word of mouth promotion that works so well in the age of social networking.

Spend some time on Facebook checking out various groups and pages to decide which one fits you better. If you're really ambitious, you might decide to use both.

Who can create a Page?

Here is another important difference between groups and pages: Anyone can start a group, but only the official representative of an organization can create a page. This goes along with Facebook's desire to make pages professional rather than personal. A page speaks for an organization itself, not for its customers or admirers. When you try to create a page, Facebook may ask for some proof that you are in fact the official representative of your organization. If you are not, Facebook suggests that you start a group rather than a page.

Once you have created your page, you can designate other people to help maintain it by making them Administrators of the page. Like a website, a page will attract more repeat visitors if you keep the content fresh and up to date.

Finding Pages and Liking them

Before you create your own Page, you will probably want to do some browsing to see what other organizations have done with their Pages—especially organizations like yours. Facebook does not give you the option to browse for pages directly from the home page of your personal profile. You need to visit page management at www.facebook.com/pages from your browser, not from Facebook's search window.

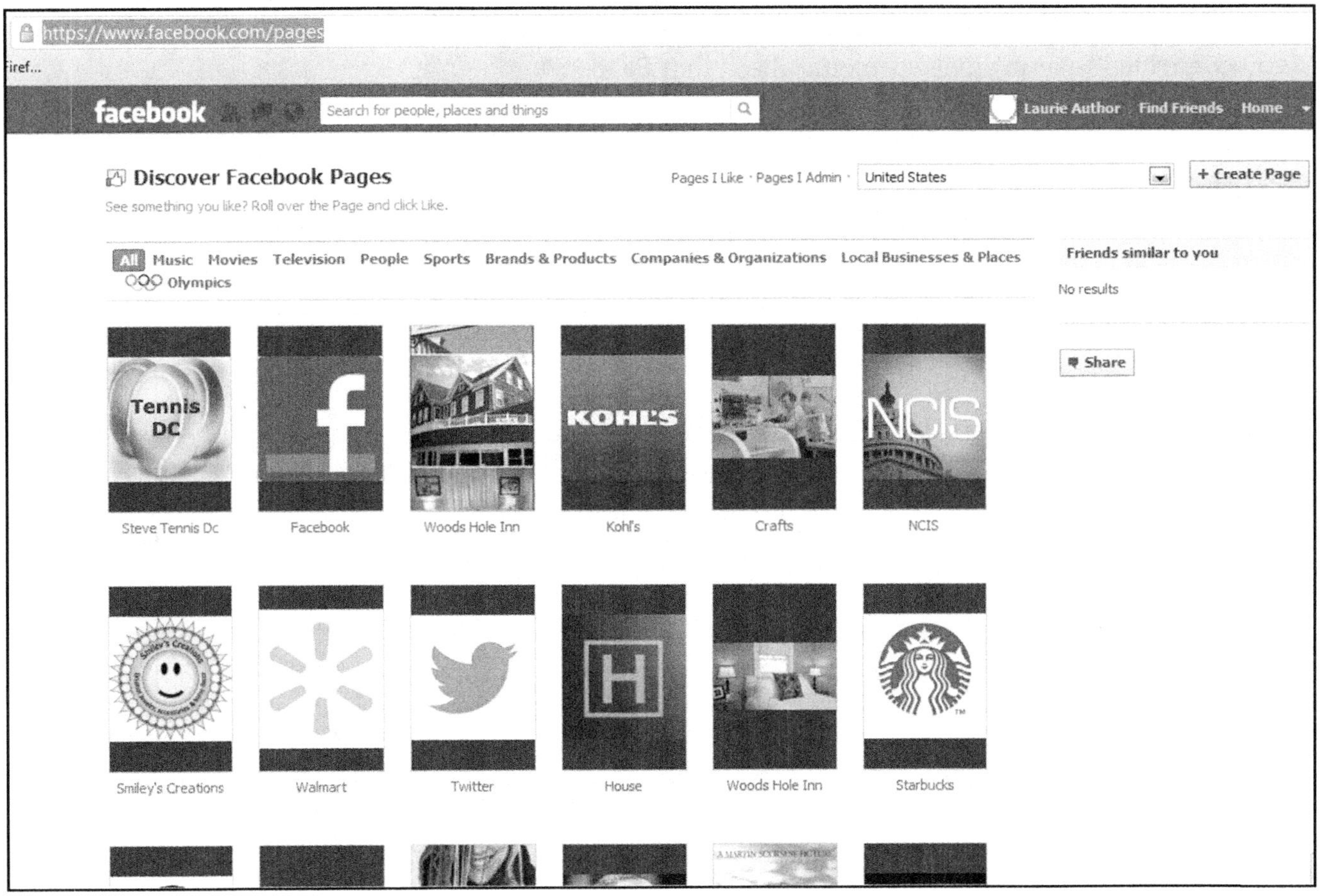

Here is where you can, as the screen says, "discover" Facebook pages. On the top right side of the page you will see two options: "Pages I Like" and "Pages I Admin." If you have already Liked pages you can click Pages I Like for a list of those. When you have created your own page or pages, they will be listed when you click on Pages I Admin.

At the top center of the page you have options to click on various categories of pages:

- All
- Music
- Movies
- Television

- People
- Sports
- Brands and Products
- Companies and Organizations
- Local Businesses and Places

When you Like a page, the page administrator cannot see your profile. This is another way in which pages are different from personal profiles. Page administrators also cannot send you an individual message, but they can respond to any messages you send to the Page, and post updates to your News Feed. Just keep in mind that when you Like a page, you are making a connection. A story about your Like will appear on your Wall (timeline) and may also appear in your news feed. You may be displayed on the Page you connected to or in advertisements about that Page.

Creating a Page

To create your own page, click on Create a Page at the bottom of any Facebook screen. Click Pages at the top of the next screen, and then click Create Page. You can also get to the Create Page screen directly by going to this address: http://www.facebook.com/pages/create.php?ref_type=sitefooter

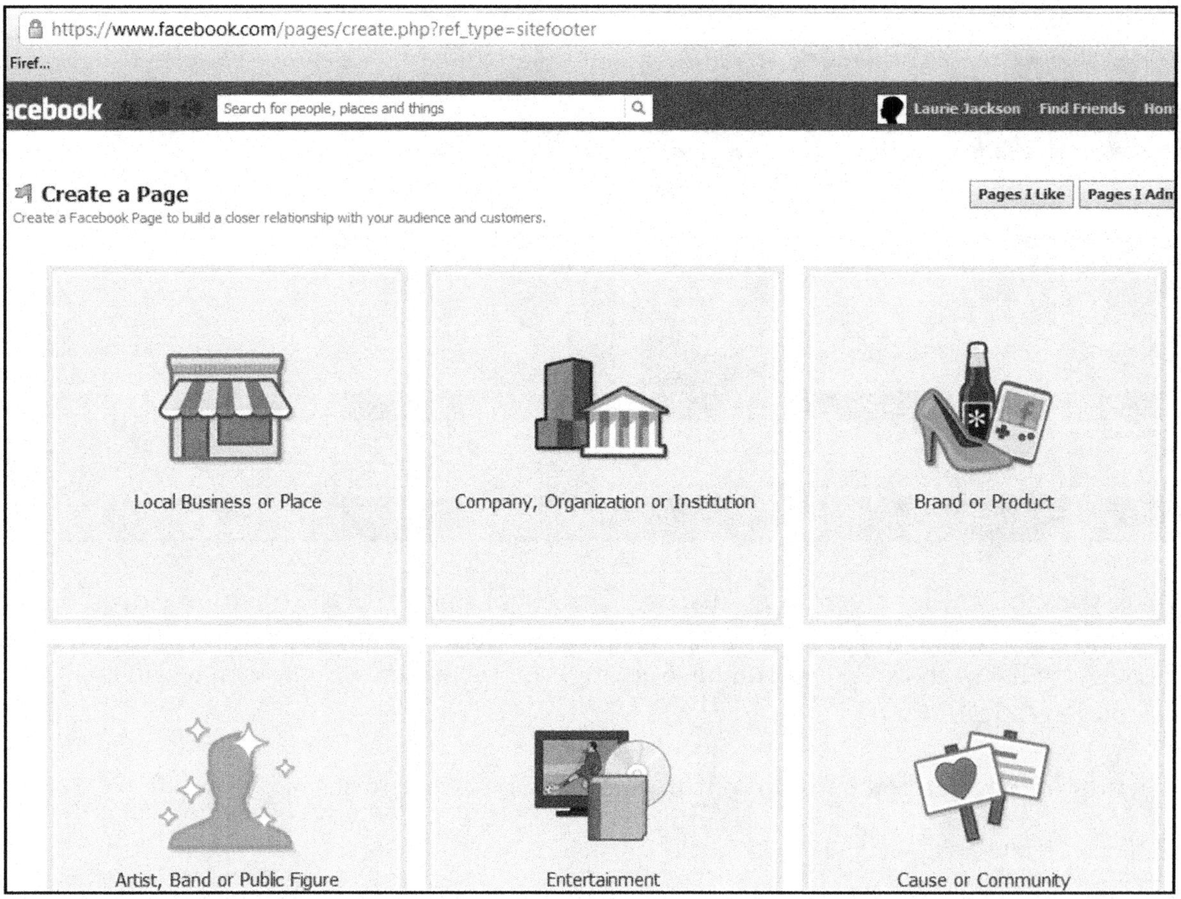

Choose the Page type that fits you:

- Local Business or Place
- Company, Organization or Institution
- Brand or Product
- Artist, Band or Public Figure
- Entertainment
- Cause or Community

Once you click on the type of Page you are creating, you will also need to choose a particular category. You must choose one of those offered, and if none is a perfect fit, you might simply choose Local Business.

Enter the name of your business. Facebook will ask you to agree to Facebook Page Terms, including certifying that you are the official representative of your organization. Be sure to read these terms carefully as it is your blueprint of what you are and are not allowed to do on your page.

Click the blue “Get Started” link and you’re ready to begin.

Notice that whenever you are on one of your Pages, not your personal profile, there is the word Voice at the top right hand side of your screen. This is to remind you that you are interacting on Facebook as your Page, rather than as you (with your personal account). Anything you post, Like, or comment on will appear on News Feeds as the name of your Page rather than you as an individual. To stop posting as your Page, click on the Home option next to the reminder to change to your personal profile.

Customizing your Page

While it’s true that a Facebook page is something like a website, there are some important differences. One of those is appearance. If you have a website, you probably gave a lot of thought to the way it looks—things like background colors, logos and eye-catching layouts. Facebook pages don’t offer you all those options. Their layout is similar to the Timeline layout of your personal profile, except that at the top of the Page there is an Admin Panel, which no one but Admins can see.

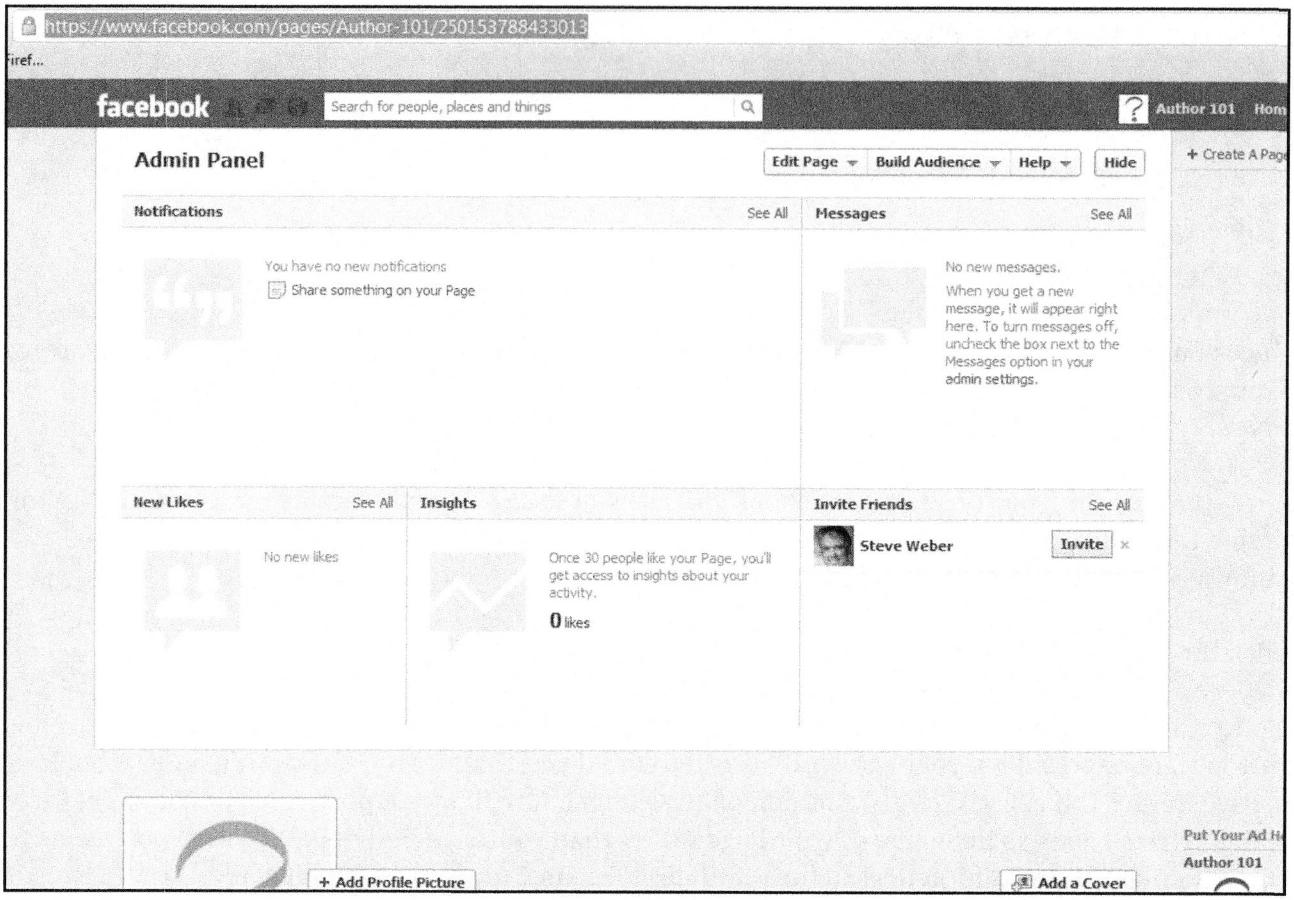

Below the Admin Panel your page begins with a profile picture and your Page Name. This layout may seem limiting to you, but it has the advantage of looking familiar to visitors. They know where to look for the information they need, and they know how to add their own comments. The key to making your page stand out is not its layout but its content. Interesting, up-to-date content will keep visitors coming back.

The photo you choose to represent your organization may be the most important thing on your page. When potential audience members browse the list of pages or search for a page on a particular topic, they will see two things: the name of your page and your photo. So it's worth spending some time choosing a photo that will give people a good idea of who you are and what you do, while at the same time creating a positive first impression.

If you have an eye-catching logo, you might decide to use that instead of a photo. The important thing to remember is that you want to create the kind of image that will make people decide to take a look at what you have to offer.

To add a photo or logo, click on the top right of the box that contains a large question mark. You can change this image later just by clicking on it.

You may also click on the small box to the right of you profile photo which says, "Add a cover." This enables you to upload a second photo to represent your business, one that will stretch across the page.

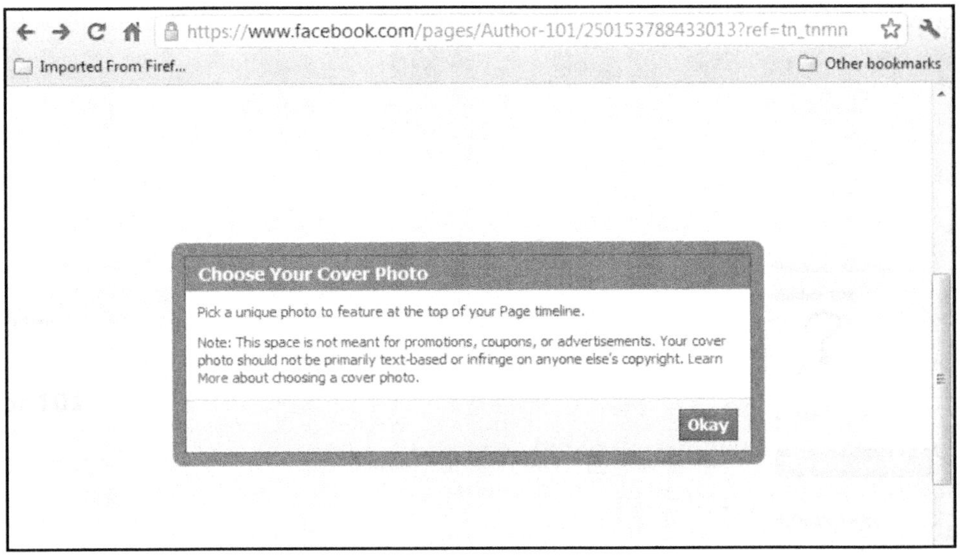

Some examples of photos you might choose to use are photos of people interacting with your product, a popular item in your line, or the cover of your most recent book. It's important to note that you may not use the Cover space for advertising sales or other promotions, or for contact information.

Below the spot for your photo, you will see a box that says, "Add Information About (the name of your organization)." Use this box to add a mission statement or a slogan. For example, "Tattoos while you wait."

Below that, you will see the standard status box on the left side of your screen, and then a box called Activity on the right side of your screen. Again, this will be familiar to you as it is similar to your personal profile.

Adding Events

Next to the "Write something" prompt box, you will see a heading for Event, Milestone +. When you click on those words you have three choices to add information about anything you have coming up that might be of interest to your users.

- Event
- Milestone
- Question

When you click on Events, a form will pop up that allows you to add:

- Event name
- Details
- Where
- When (date) and time

There are also two boxes to check to enable you to show the guest list, and to specify that only Page Admins may post about the event. Events can be important or trivial, large or small. The purpose of adding something here is to let people know that your organization is active and vibrant. You always have something going on.

Adding other information

You can add information to your page in basically the same way you add information to your personal profile. Use the status box to post news, photos or video of anything that you think will interest the people who Like your page. For example:

- If you own a restaurant and you plan to start serving a Sunday brunch buffet, add an announcement about it.
- If your band is going to be playing in a local club, tell people when and where.
- If you are going to have a booth at an upcoming trade show, invite people to stop by and say hello.
- If you own a garden store and you just received a shipment of Japanese maples, tell people to visit you to check out the foliage.

Writing on your wall is your main method to let people know what's going on in your organization. You don't need to wait for a major event or milestone to post something to your wall. Instead, think about what people who Like your page might find interesting. Suppose you own a bicycle shop and you come across an article in the newspaper about the growing popularity of recumbent bikes (the kind you sit on like a recliner). If you sell recumbent bikes, you could write a sentence or two on your wall about the article and invite people to visit your store to see these unusual contraptions for themselves. You can also use the postings on your wall to add links to sites that will provide more information.

People who Like your page can write on your wall in the same way that your friends can write on the wall of your personal profile, and you can set up your permissions in much the same way as you do on your personal profile. Click on the words "Edit Page" at the top right hand side of your Page, then click on Manage Permissions.

Most will write nice things on your wall. (If they didn't like your business, why would they have Liked your page?) Sometimes though, someone who is disgruntled, or just someone with poor taste, will post an offensive comment. You can easily delete those, and if the problem continues, you can permanently block the offending person from posting. To remove the comment, hover over the right corner of their comment until the "x" appears. You can then click on the "x" to delete it, and you are given the option to delete and ban the user at the same time. Although this type of problem is rare, it's a good reason to check your page often to make sure nothing objectionable appears there.

About: Click on Edit Page on the top right of the screen and then Update Info. You can use this form to list all pertinent information, including your address, phone number, and hours of operation. If you decide some of the boxes on this form are irrelevant, just leave them blank. The information you enter on these forms will be displayed under the top banner of your page, below your photo.

Photos: Under your banner, to the right of About, is a space for your photos. Click on the word Photo and then the box "Add Photo" to create a photo album to show off what you have to offer. If you own a banquet facility, you could use photos of your dining room arranged for different kinds of events. If you run a dog-walking business, you could include photos of yourself with some of your canine customers. You can also allow your users to post photos on your page. If you use this option, your users' photos will appear in a separate section from yours, so that people will be able to distinguish between your photos and theirs.

The last item on your Admin Panel is a handy box called Page Tips, a running list of ways you can build and engage your audience. To see all the tips at once, click on Resources on the left menu of the Update Info page. If you're a stand-up comedian, you could add Apps such as Video so that you could upload your latest hilarious performance. If you're a musician, you can add a Music Player to give users access to all or part of one of your songs.

Use Social Plug-ins: On the list of Resources, you can take advantage of a great list of easy-to-add social plug in features to your own blog or business website (not your Facebook page) so that things you post there are easily shared on Facebook. For more information on this, see Chapter 13.

Ready, set, publish!

Once you have your page basically the way you want it, click Publish This Page at the top of the page editing screen. Later, if for some reason you do not want your page to be available for a while, you can unpublish it by clicking on Settings, on the editing screen. You can also use Settings to set age limit restrictions on your page, if you think that is appropriate.

8 ► PROMOTING AND MONITORING YOUR PAGE

Once your Facebook page is published, you can start telling the world about it. Invite, invite, invite. Facebook makes it easy for you to send an invitation to Like your page to all your friends; just click on Build Audience in your Admin Panel and you can invite email contacts and all your Facebook friends.

If you already have a website, you can post an announcement there inviting people to visit your page. Many people use Facebook every day. Once these folks become users of your Facebook page, they will probably use it—rather than your website—as their primary source of information about your business

If you have an email list of customers and other people who have expressed an interest in your business, you can use that to get out the word about your page. If you decide to do this, don't bury the announcement in a message about some other topic. It's a good general rule that each email message should be about just one thing. If you try to tell people half a dozen things in one message, you can't be confident that anything will sink in.

If you decide to use email to announce the debut of your page, it's probably best to send just one message to the people on your list. It's true that in advertising, repetition is essential to getting your point across, but email works a little differently. Repeated email messages on the same topic can be annoying. They can also lead people to assign all of your messages a low priority, or even tune them out altogether.

Be sure to add a link to your Facebook page in the signature line of your emails.

Of course, if you own a physical store, you can tell customers about your Facebook page in person. You might also put a sign in your window or print a note automatically at the bottom of your receipts. Some of your customers will just ignore this kind of announcement, but people who are devoted Facebook users—and their numbers are growing daily—will probably view your page, maybe just out of curiosity. If they view your page once, they will probably become fans, since it only takes one click. Once they become users, their friends will see your page listed on their profiles, and they might become users, too. If you keep your page interesting and you have something worthwhile to sell, your user base will keep growing with minimal effort on your part. And it all started with a sign in your store window.

You can also start the process of building a user base by using your page itself. At the upper right side of your page, click on Build and Audience, and then choose Share Page. You can use this feature to send a message about your page to as your friends or your previously established groups; you can also post a message about your Page on a particular friends' Wall. Again, it is probably not a good idea to send this type of message more than once to each person on your list. You want to let people know about your page, but you don't want to be annoying.

Consider relationships you might have with other businesses–perhaps complementary businesses or providers of services that you use–and how you can mutually benefit one another using Facebook. They can become users of your page, and vice versa, so that your content appears on both of your News Feeds. This can effectively drive new business both ways.

Use resources already at your disposal. Do you belong to a trade group that already has a Facebook presence? Find out how your page can interact with it. Do you use a venue (online or otherwise) for selling that already has Facebook promotion groups, such as Etsy? Get in on them. Search Facebook for networking groups; they might not be the very best quality Likes you can get for your page, but they are a start.

Facebook has made it easy for page admins to keep track of where they have visited and commented and Liked other pages by accessing the Activity Log. You will find it on your Admin Panel by clicking on the Edit Page box at the top of the page. Click on Use Activity Log and you (and only you) will see a list of everything your page has done, by date.

You can also use your Facebook page as a resource with a bricks-and-mortar business, even if you don't already have a Facebook presence. For example, if you'd like to place business cards or flyers about your business or event at local business or shop, tell them you'll Like their page from your Facebook page in exchange for letting you leave them. If they don't have a Facebook page, tell them you'll post a one-time status update along the lines of, "Pick up our flyer at the Ding Dong Shop on 3rd and West Avenue." Every business understands the value of a Facebook mention.

If you want to take the process of promoting your page once step further, and you don't mind spending a little money, you can use a Facebook ad to get the word out. (You can learn more about advertising in the next chapter.) The advantage of advertising your page on Facebook is that people who see your ad are already Facebook users, and they know how easy it is to view a page without going to a new website or losing track of where they were.

Keep people coming back

Pages are like websites. Visitors will keep coming back if you make the content rich and you update it frequently. One of the advantages of a Facebook page, as opposed to a website, is that you need no special expertise to add new information or photos. You also don't need to wait for major events or developments in your business to add new content. Updating your page is so simple that you can add information whenever you think of something that might be interesting to your users. Inspire them, and share knowledge that will keep people engaged in your page. And your users can add new content by commenting on your posts and writing reviews.

Everyone likes a special deal. It is easy to give your users value by offering them something that is exclusive to them as Facebook users. Offer an extra free item with a purchase, or a percentage off, simply by posting it on your Facebook page. Perhaps "Like us on Facebook and get a free drink with your sandwich on your next visit." If you sell online, offer a coupon code that works with your checkout system to discount the price.

If your business is smaller, you can easily manage via the honor system without worrying about people taking unfair advantage of your offer. A local taco restaurant offers a 10% discount if you check in while you're ordering and then show your mobile screen to the cashier. They don't mind if you do it over and over again, because it's great advertising for them, for the price.

Facebook is currently testing Offers, which is an easy way to create coupons from pages. Similar to creating an Event, it is a quick menu that allows you to make a business offer, specify how many times users may redeem it, and add other terms and conditions such as an expiration date. When Facebook makes it available to all page admins, you will see it as an option in next to Event, Milestone + on your page's status bar.

One of the easiest ways to update your page is to add new photos. People love looking at photos. One of the reasons for Facebook's success is that it makes it so easy to share photo albums. In general, photos of people are more interesting than photos of products. If you make jewelry, you might use photos of your friends wearing some of your latest creations, along with close-up shots of the jewelry itself. If you own a restaurant, you might use photos of your friendly wait staff in action. If you own a dog grooming business, you might use photos of your satisfied customers—the four-legged kind, that is.

You can also add some "news value" to your page by announcing events. Sponsoring events is an effective marketing approach in itself. If you own a bookstore, you might sponsor a monthly discussion meeting for mystery users. If you own any kind of business with a good-sized parking lot, you might let a high school group use it to hold a car wash as a fund raiser. Events like these have marketing value in themselves, but they also give you something you can add to the Events listing on your page. And once you have held the event, you can add photos of it to your album.

Your page makes it easy for you to talk about your business. When a user writes on your wall or contributes to a discussion board, post a friendly, positive reply, even if the user says something negative. Remember that everything you add to your page contributes, for better or worse, to the image people have of your business.

Use your blog to promote your Facebook page...

Maybe you already have a blog or website for your business and you think a Facebook page is a duplication of effort. It's not. Set up your Facebook page as just another online presence, and use the page to simply drive Facebook traffic back where you want it, like your blog. There are a couple of easy ways to do this:

A Page Badge: Facebook makes it easy for you to add a badge with the name of your Facebook page to your blog or website. You can generate the code and then copy it and add it to your blog layout. It will show up as a small box in Facebook blue and when users click on it, they are linked directly to your page. To create one, click on Add Badge to Your Site in the bottom left sidebar of your homepage, then choose the option Page Badges.

A Like Box: This plug-in allows website users to see information from your Facebook page's news feed, including recent posts and the number of users who already Like it. There is a Like button they can click to Like your page directly from your blog or website–without ever needing to visit the Page.

...and vice versa

Publish directly from your blog to your Facebook page. There are several applications you can download onto your Facebook page that will post your blogs directly to your page, automatically. When you post on your blog, that blog post publishes to Facebook without you having to do anything else. One of the most popular ones is called Networked Blogs.

You can also set up your Facebook page so that all your status updates automatically publish to your Twitter account.

Facebook also gives you a way to make it easy for others to share your blog or website content to their Facebook pages. There are Social Plug-in applications found on the Facebook Platform that enable you to do just that. You can add a Like Button, which lets users share something on your site back to their Facebook profile with just one click. There is also a plug-in that allows users to send your website or blog content to their Facebook friends. For more information about what's available on the Facebook Platform, see Chapter 13.

Use YouTube to promote your Facebook Page

If you have your own channel on YouTube, you can use their feature Connect Accounts to link to your Facebook Page. Then people who are viewing your YouTube channel can click on it and visit your page.

Using Insights

Facebook Insights give you just that: valuable insights into how people are using and responding to your page. Once you reach 30 Likes, the data increases so that you can even see demographics of those who have Liked your page. You can access your Page Insights from your Admin Panel. It is the second to last block.

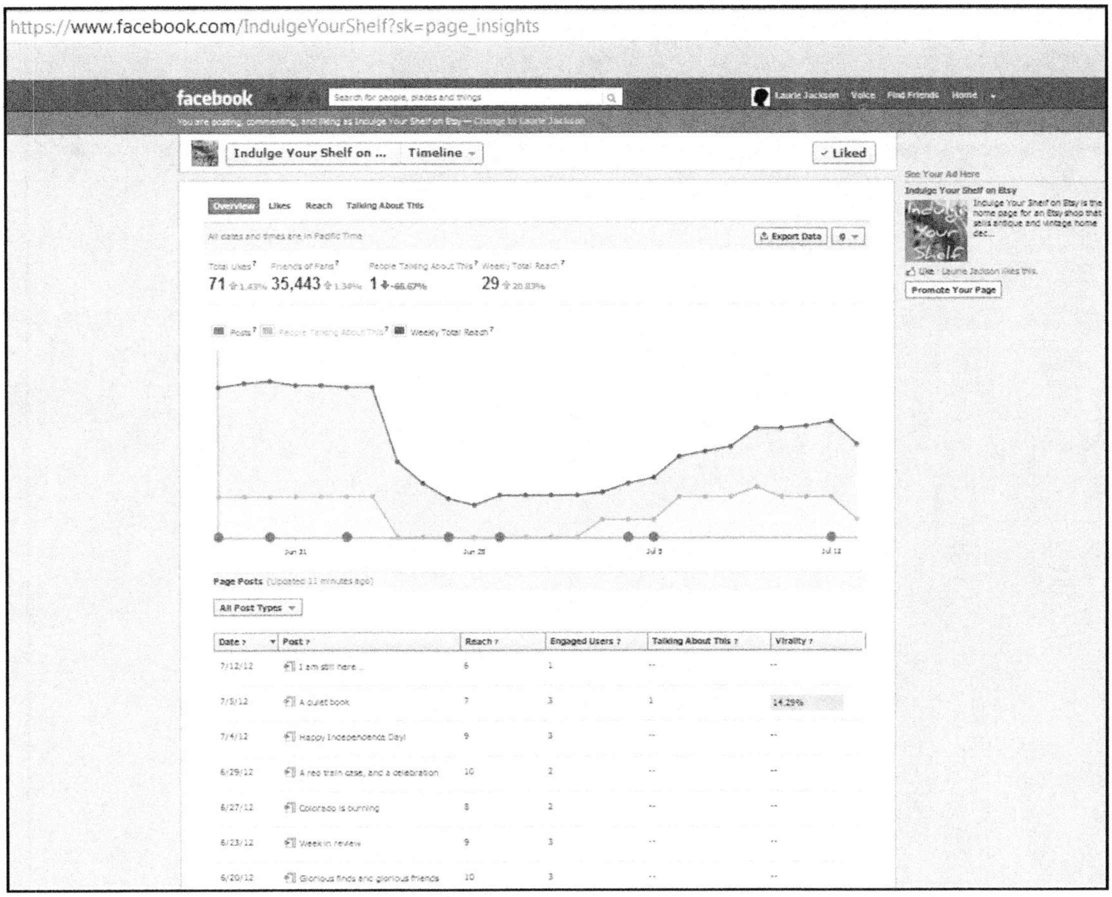

Here is what Insights offers:

An overview of interactions: This includes any sort of interaction users have with your page—writing on your wall, commenting on your posts, or liking your content.

People Who Like Your Page: If you have at least 30 Likes you will see demographics (gender, age) and location of people who Like your page.

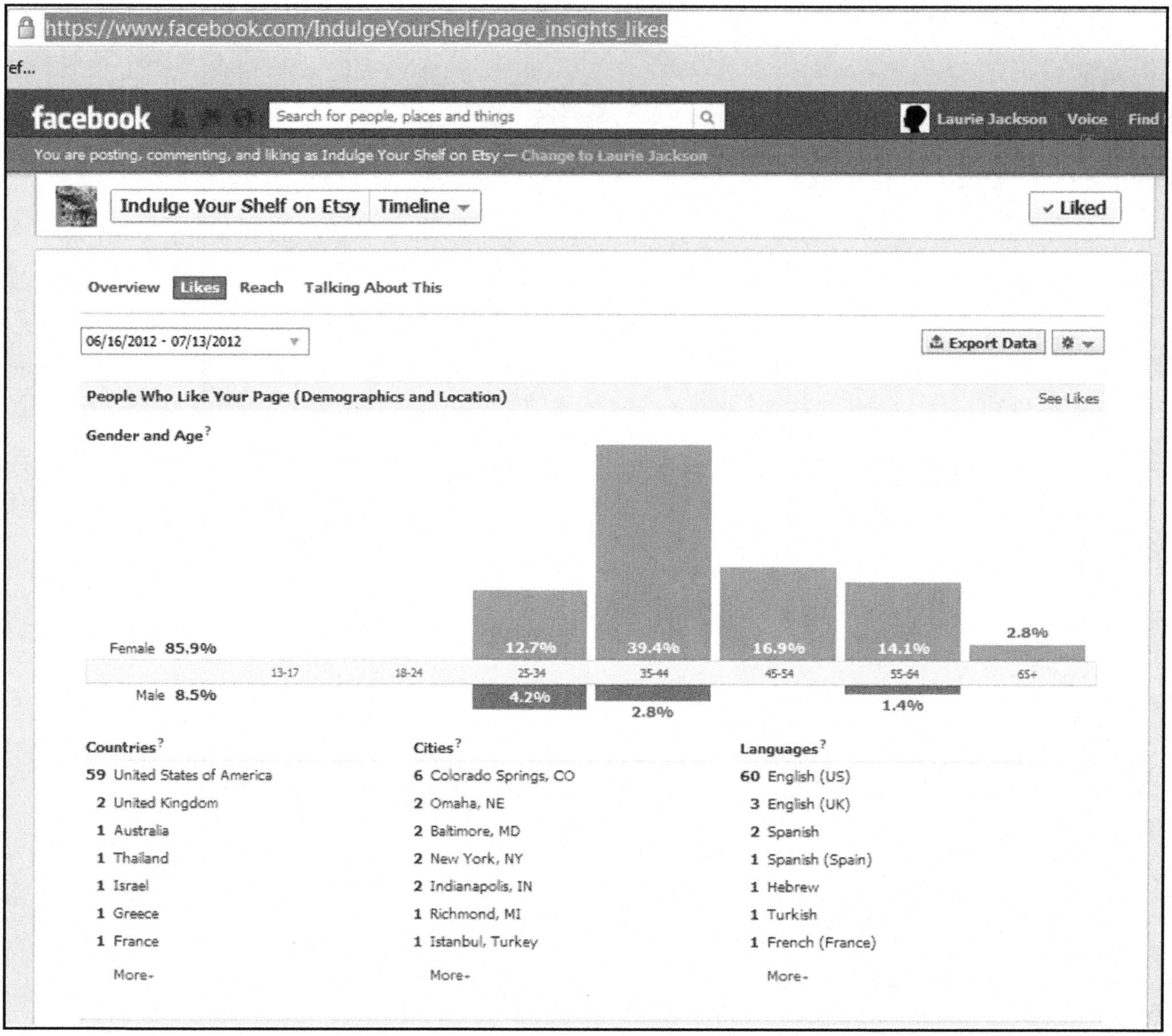

- **Reach:** You can see how you reached people in the following ways:

1. **Organically:** People who saw your content in News Feed, including people who have Liked your page and those who haven't
2. **Paid:** People who saw an Ad or Sponsored Story
3. **Viral:** People who saw a story because one of their Friends Liked it, posted to your Page's wall, or shared one of your Page's posts
4. **Page Views:** Broken down by actual views and then unique views
5. **How People are Talking About Your Page:** How content on your page was shared.
6. **Post Quality:** You can gauge the performance of each of your individual posts—their reach, the number of people they engaged, and how many talked about it. Posts are also given a "Virality" score, which tells you the percentage of people who have created a story out of your Page post from the number of people who have seen it.

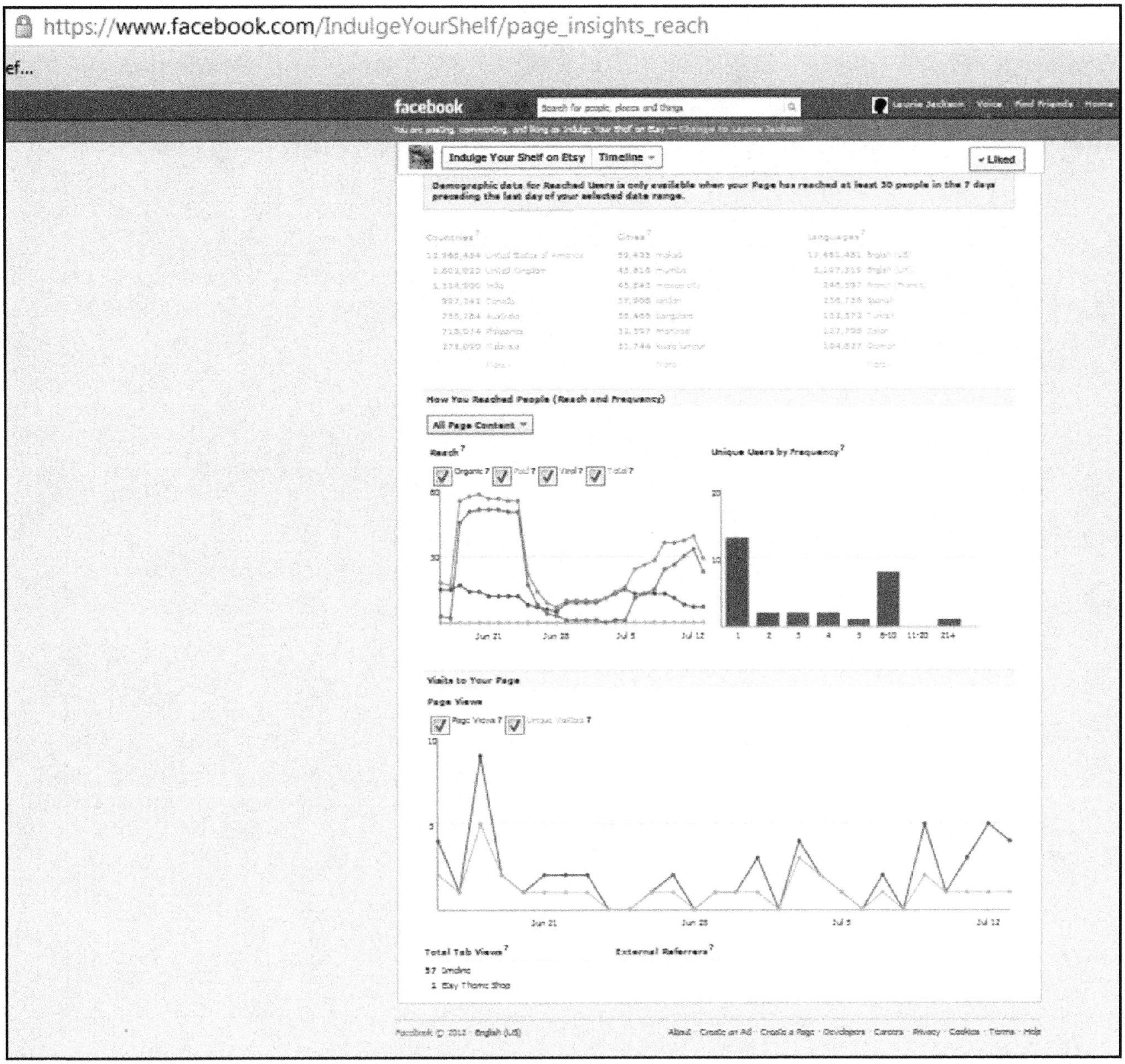

You can use the tools provided by Insights to gain a better understanding of what's working and what isn't working in terms of promoting your page. For example, suppose you bought a Facebook ad to promote your page, but you saw no significant increase in your total number of users. You might decide the ad was not worthwhile. Or suppose you added a post about a new product or service and your user interactions tripled. You would know that you were probably onto something good.

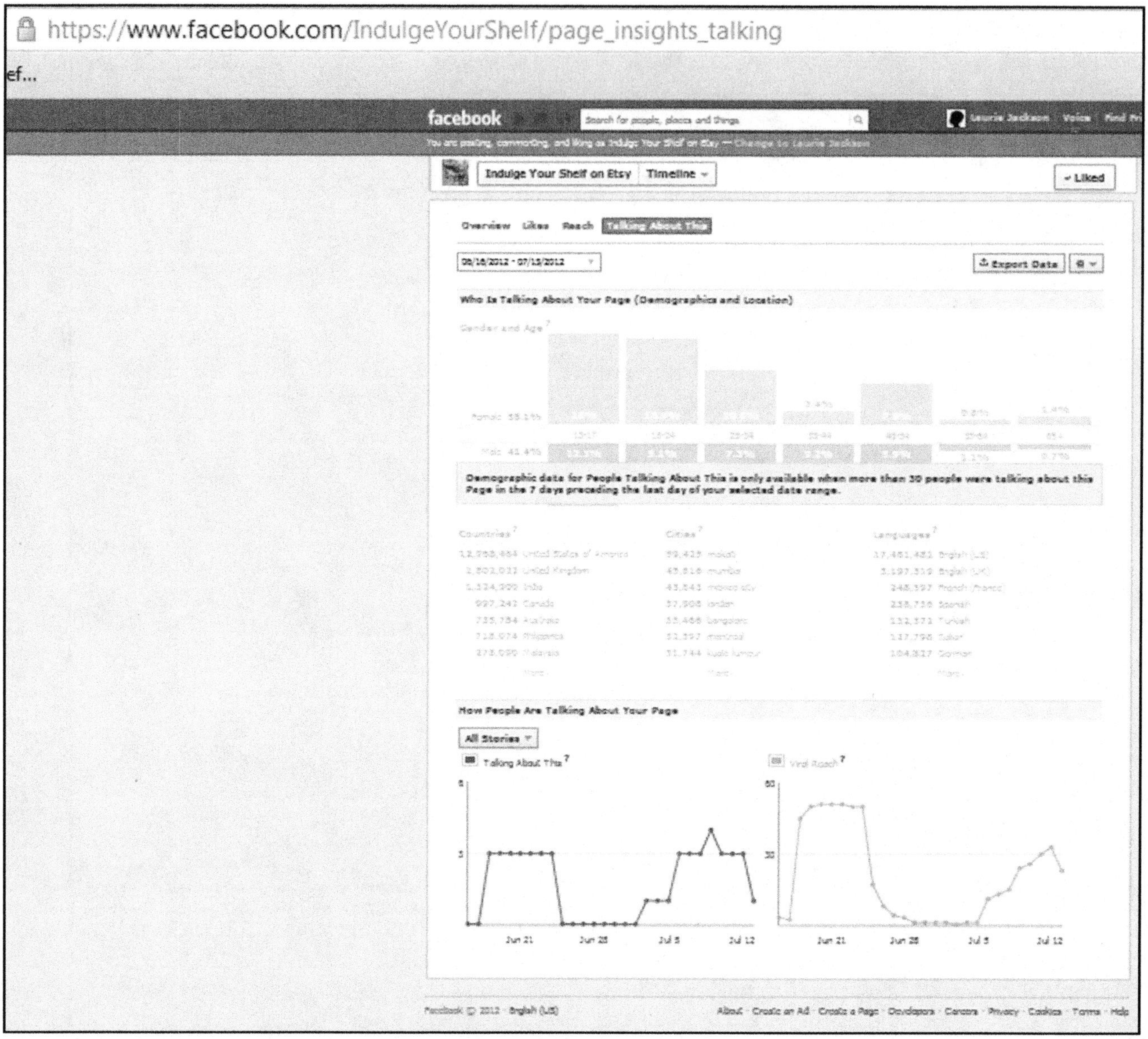

A success story: the Rothbury Festival

In 2008, music entrepreneurs AEG Live and Madison House joined forces to create a new festival in Michigan over the Fourth of July weekend. One of their first steps to promote the festival was to create a Facebook page loaded with information about the event. Then they bought some Facebook ads to drive people to the page. The day the ads launched, the number of new users added each day tripled. The Facebook friends of these users learned about the Rothbury page and many of them became fans, too. Rothbury has gone to become a tremendous success for everyone involved.

9 ► FACEBOOK EVENTS

Since Facebook is devoted to social networking, it's not surprising that it offers a convenient way to plan social events—or any other kind of event that you might have in mind. If you ever hold events to promote your business, you can use the Events function to publicize them and attract more customers. But before we look at that, let's see what Facebook Events is all about.

Finding and viewing Events

To see how the Events function works, begin by clicking the little calendar page icon on the left sidebar of any Facebook screen. The default view is list mode. In list mode you will see small calendars of the current month and following month on the left side of your screen. On the right side of the screen are boxes for Today, and below that any other notable upcoming dates which have an event associated with them, such as the birthdays of your Friends, events you have been invited to, and events you have said you will attend. This also shows events that your friends have said they will attend, and it gives you an opportunity to join in those by clicking Join from this very screen

You can also click on Calendar to get a full screen of the current month which lists all your events, even past ones in the current month. If you use the Facebook Mobile App, it will show the mobile Check-Ins you might have posted on your wall on the given day.

There are two ways to view past events. When you are in the list view, click any of the bolded dates on the calendar to see all events that happened that day. If a date is not bolded, there was no event on that day. To view a previous month's events, hover over the small calendar and click "View Month." Then use the arrows to jump to previous months. In calendar view, events that happened in the current month will still appear on your calendar. To view events that happened earlier in the year, click the link to the previous month that appears above the calendar.

If you're new to Facebook, you will probably have nothing scheduled, but you might find your calendar full anyway, with Friends' Events and birthdays.

If you would just like to see what an event listing looks like, you can use the search feature to find something that might interest you. If you can't think of anything, search for "Star Trek," and then click on the Search Filter on the left sidebar for Events. Click on the magnifying glass in the search bar to bring up the search filter. You will be shown a list of past and upcoming meetings and conventions. Click on one that looks promising. You will find all the information you need about the event, including the host, location, date and time, event description, contact information, links and confirmed guests. You will also have an opportunity to RSVP (if the event is open) and to share the event information with other Facebook users.

Create an Event

Businesses have long recognized the marketing value of sponsoring events. Large corporations sponsor golf tournaments and college bowl games. Small local companies sponsor chili cook-offs and road races. No matter what business you're in, you can probably think of some type of event that will shine a spotlight on your organization. Facebook adds to the promotional value of sponsoring an event by announcing what you're doing to the whole world—or at least your little corner of it.

Before you create an event on Facebook, you should have a definite plan. At a minimum, you should know what the event will involve and where and when it will be held.

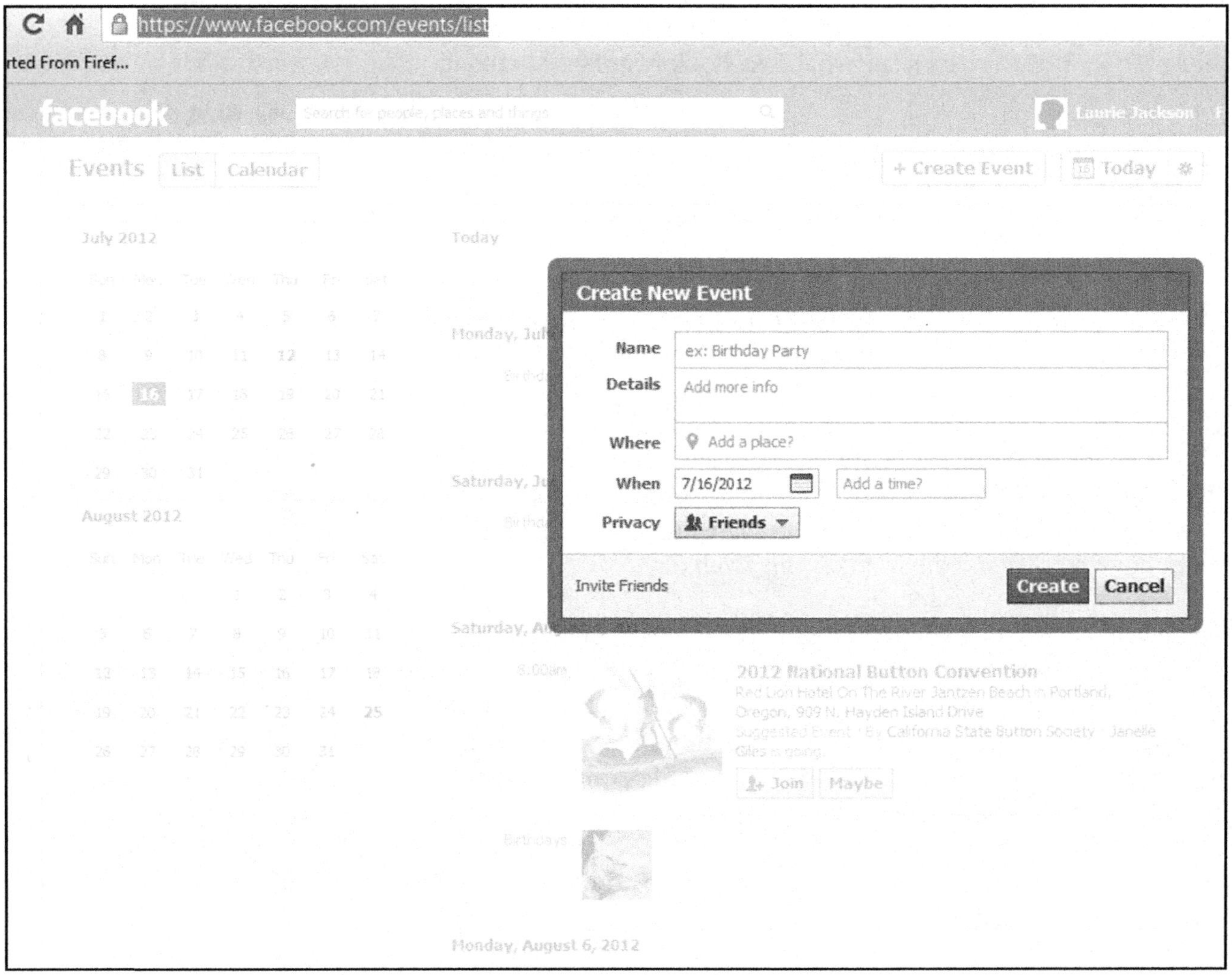

To begin announcing your Event on Facebook, click the little calendar icon on the left sidebar of any Facebook screen. This will bring you to the main Events screen. Click the Create an Event box on the top right of the screen to get started.

Step 1: Event Info

- **Name:** For example, "Monroe Gallery's Grand Re-Opening"

- **Details:** A brief description of your event. Obviously you want to make the event sound as appealing as possible. You should make the description as clear and accurate as possible so that people won't be disappointed if the event turns out to be different from what they expected.
- **Where:** The name of your physical site, for example, The Monroe Gallery
- **When:** Date and time of your event. When you create the event, there is only a box for the start time. An end time box will appear as an option only after you click on Create Event; you can click on Edit later from the event page itself to add an end time.
- **Privacy:** This is where you decide who can see your invitation. Your choices are:
  - **Friends:** Only people who have Liked your page
  - **Public:** Your event will show up when anyone on Facebook searches for an event like this. Since your objective is to publicize your business, you will probably want to choose this option.
  - **Invite Only:** From here you can choose whether invited guests can invite their friends, and whether or not you wish all invitees to be able to see the guest list.

When you have finished, click Create Event and you will be taken to a new page dedicated just to your event.

Step 2: Customize your event

- **Upload a picture:** Try to come up with one good picture to represent your event. This will be displayed at the top left of your event page. If you don't upload a picture, that position on your event page will display a large calendar icon.

Step 3: Invite Friends

If you didn't already send invitations when you were creating the event, you can do so now. Select guests from a list of your Facebook friends or send an email invitation to anyone else you choose. You can also add a personal message to the invitation. When your list is complete, click "Send Invitations." You can always invite more people later.

Managing an Event

Once your event page is up and running, there are several ways you can use it to manage your event. You can:

- **Send a message to all guests.**
- **View and manage your guest list.** You can promote a guest to become an administrator of the event or ban a guest from the event permanently. You might choose to ban a guest if he is posting offensive content on the wall of the event page.
- **Change the event information.** For example, hours or location.
- **Promote the event non-stop until it takes place.** You might highlight a different aspect of the event every couple of days, such as talent and/or vendors who will be on hand. Write a note about them and post on your Facebook page, or do a status update with a link to your own website's post about them. Be sure to send a link to the event to the Facebook pages of the talent,

vendors, or people involved in your event—and try sharing it on the pages of other business contacts. This is how you create "buzz" about the event.

Is there something happening in the news that relates to your event? Draw attention to that on your event page. For example, if your business is in the fashion industry and a hit television show that focuses on fashion is starting their new season Thursday night, mention it on your event page that week. Your users will enjoy the information (they might have forgotten about the series opener and now they'll remember to record it), and it creates a positive association between your event and the hit show.

During an Event

In the days and hours leading up to the event, create excitement by posting photos of the set-up, the beautiful weather you'll be having, and even guests as they are arriving.

Continue to post photos and status updates during the event, like "Come on down," to remind prospective guests it's not too late to join in the fun. If you'll be too busy to do this yourself, ask someone to help you.

After the Event

Your event page remains active after the event. This allows you and your guests to post photos and make comments about what a great time everyone had. If you think you will be too busy during your event to take photos, ask someone else to do it. People who attended the event will enjoy visiting the event page to browse photo albums.

Success Story: Free Slurpee Day

Every year, a number of 7-Eleven stores sponsor 7-Eleven Day on July 11 (7/11). Customers can receive a free small slurpee, the signature drink of the convenience store chain. As long as they are there, customers often buy snacks to go with their slurpees. The company has created an Event page on Facebook to promote 7-Eleven Day. In 2012, the event had over 42,000 confirmed guests.

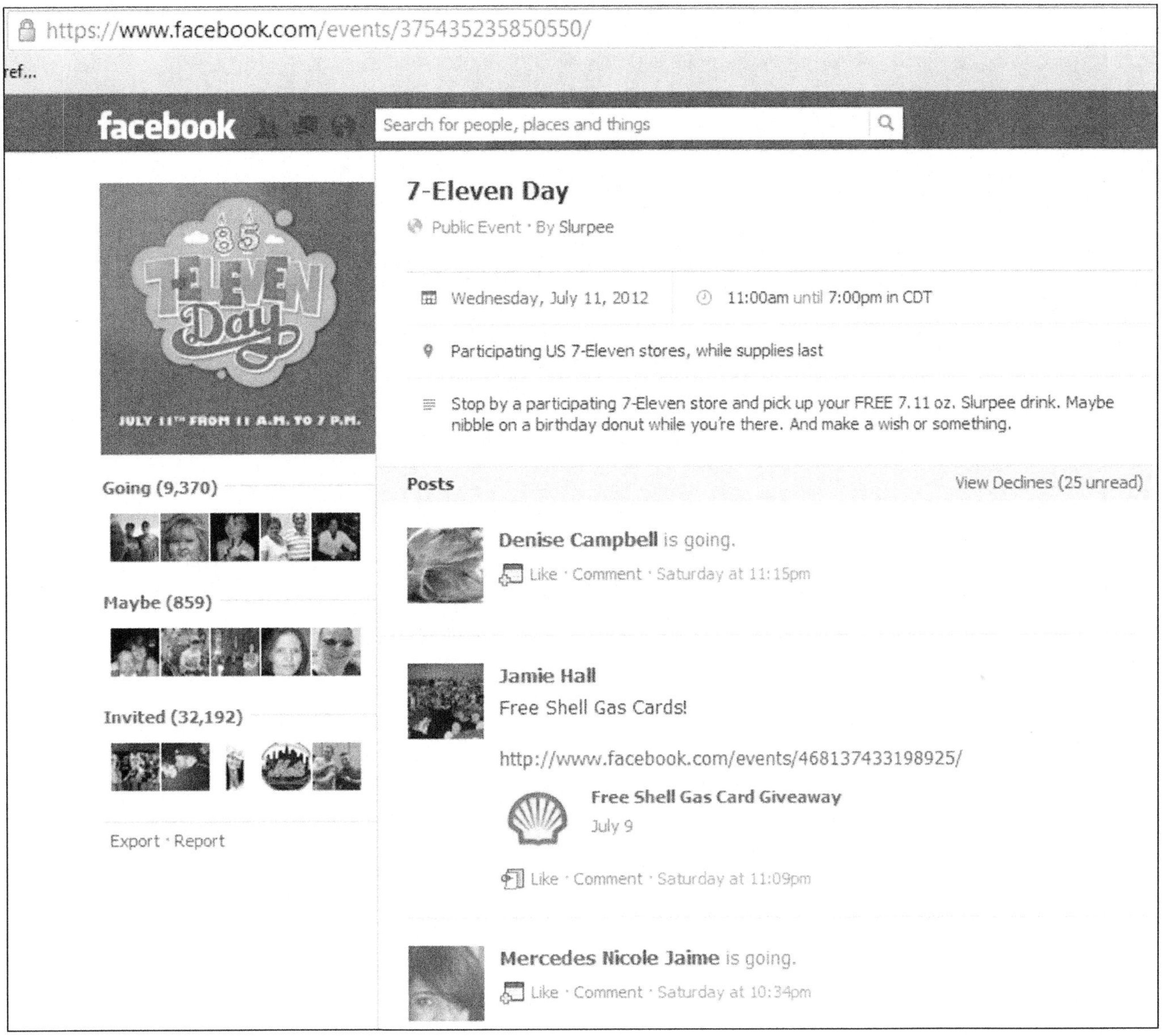
https://www.facebook.com/events/375435235850550/
facebook
Search for people, places and things
7-Eleven Day
Public Event · By Slurpee
Wednesday, July 11, 2012
11:00am until 7:00pm in CDT
Participating US 7-Eleven stores, while supplies last
Stop by a participating 7-Eleven store and pick up your FREE 7.11 oz. Slurpee drink. Maybe nibble on a birthday donut while you're there. And make a wish or something.
JULY 11TH FROM 11 A.M. TO 7 P.M.
Going (9,370)
Maybe (859)
Invited (32,192)
Export · Report
Posts
View Declines (25 unread)
Denise Campbell is going.
Like · Comment · Saturday at 11:15pm
Jamie Hall
Free Shell Gas Cards!
http://www.facebook.com/events/468137433198925/
Free Shell Gas Card Giveaway
July 9
Like · Comment · Saturday at 11:09pm
Mercedes Nicole Jaime is going.
Like · Comment · Saturday at 10:34pm

10 ▶ PAID ADVERTISING ON FACEBOOK

We've already looked at a multitude of ways to leverage Facebook without paying a dime and how many successful promoters never exhaust the free mileage they obtain from grassroots Facebook efforts.

Now we're entering the realm of paid advertising. And paid advertising carries with it some risk. To put it plainly, if you spend a lot of money on advertising without knowing what you're doing, you can easily go broke.

So here are some caveats about paid advertising:

Don't pay for advertising before your business is up and running for at least one year. First, you must understand your customer base, how they find you, and how they decide to buy from you instead of someone else. You've got to know your costs, what a customer is worth to you, and how much you can afford to pay for ads. Remember, many entrepreneurs don't need paid advertising at all—they've got all the business they can handle. Their customers happily do their advertising for them—through Facebook Likes and word of mouth.

Be patient. It's tempting to plop down a wad of cash for ads. For a moment, buying ads feels great; it feels like you're taking bold action to jump-start your business. In reality, there probably are other reasons that sales are slow—your products or services aren't in high demand, or the niche you're targeting is oversupplied. Businesses never starve from lack of advertising; they die from a lack of customers.

Pay only for what you can measure. If you're going to pay for advertising, pay only for what you can measure. Know exactly how many sales and new customers your advertising dollars are bringing in. Is your profit margin less than $20 or $30 per item, like many entrepreneurs? Then your new customers are unlikely to pay for any advertising that will make a noticeable difference in your sales.

In any event, advertising is a whole new can of worms. It's an investment. It's risk. And whenever you're making a big investment, you must have YOUR bottom line ruling your decisions. And that's why you can't do paid advertising at first—you don't even know what your bottom line is yet!

It's sad but true: A lot of advertising programs—perhaps most small ad buys—are sold to suckers whose money is wasted. If you're risking your money, make sure you're getting results for your dollars.

Can paid advertising work with your business? Probably. But it's most likely to work when you have an established business with two key characteristics:

High price points and high profit margins - If your items sell for $100 or $200, and your profit margins exceed 40 percent, you might be able to make the advertising pay. It's possible. If your price points are about $20, forget it.

A proven customer list - Let's say you've been in business for four years. You've got a customer list of about 1,000 people who spend an average of $250 with you, year after year. Those are repeat customers. Now you should have some cash you can risk toward advertising because you know that acquiring a new customer brings in an average $250 in sales annually.

Will paid Facebook ads pay off for your business?

For many businesses, paid ads on Facebook are the most cost- and time-effective way to raise awareness for your business and reach the greatest number of new customers.

If you're a B2C (business-to-consumer) organization, like most businesses, you sell goods or services directly to the public. B2C businesses have the most to gain from well-run Facebook ad campaigns because much of their customer base is already on Facebook. Some examples of these organizations would be:

- A company trying to sell their goods or services online to the general public
- Any brick and mortar or physical retail business that doesn't primarily sell to other companies
- Artists or musicians looking to promote themselves

On the other hand, if you're a B2B (business-to-business) company targeting larger firms, you might have a tough time reaching customers on Facebook. Business decision-makers in larger organizations rarely consult online social networks when looking for a new supplier, no matter what you're offering. Many corporate worksites and schools block Facebook usage on their networks—perhaps on the theory that workers would waste too much time socializing instead of working.

However, if you're a B2B provider targeting Mom-and-Pop operators and home businesses, Facebook ads might be valuable for you. These businesses are often sole-proprietorships or independently owned, and the person in charge of purchasing decisions might be one of the "always working" types. They might use Facebook primarily for personal reasons, while also on the lookout for ways to improve their business. With savvy use of Facebook's ad platform, "Choose Your Audience," you can intuitively target the site's users that will likely fit this demographic and ensure that your ad gets to the small start-ups and entrepreneurs.

In summary, if you're selling to consumers, Facebook ads are a strong possibility for finding new customers. If you're selling to businesses, the answer isn't so definite. But if you're in the business of selling to other small businesses, Facebook ads are worth a try.

Getting started with Facebook Ads

While savvy management of your profile and its social aspects are an undoubtedly important part of your marketing mix, it's only half of what Facebook has to offer. Combined with the organic publicity methods we've discussed in the earlier portions of this book, Facebook contributes to an unparalleled combination of viral marketing.

Over the past couple of years, Facebook's paid ad campaign system has become one of the Internet's most full featured, and for many types of businesses, its most effective. Facebook has developed an affordable, easy-to-understand, and measurable system that even the smallest of businesses can buy into and see results from quickly.

Here's a view of Facebook while I'm logged into my personal profile. I've circled the paid ads in the right sidebar. Each ad is targeted toward me, based on Facebook pages my friends and I Like. Businesses sponsor these ads on a pay-per-click basis (typically 30 cents to a few dollars per click) or a cost-per-thousand impressions (CPM) basis.

The right sidebar of most Facebook pages displays a column of Facebook ads. Not only do these ads allow you to lure potential customers, but you can incorporate them into your marketing plan and bolster your free Facebook marketing efforts. Most importantly, Facebook ads allow you to target the site's users that will have the greatest chance at responding to your ad, and ultimately become your customers.

Getting started and posting your first ad can be an intimidating proposition, especially if you're not extremely familiar with the site already. Fortunately, it isn't a "technical" process at all. Facebook's ad system is much easier and more intuitive than alternatives such as Google Adwords, for example. So let's get started.

Why are paid Facebook Ads so powerful?

Facebook's paid ad platform has unique features, and the following six points illustrate why it's become the best possible advertising investment that most small businesses can make.

Everyone's on Facebook (almost). The foundation of any successful paid ad campaign, online or offline, is the ability to reach a high number of potential customers. In the past, the only choices of paid ads for small business owners were newspapers, magazines, large global ad networks (like Google Adwords), business directories such as YellowPages.com, local radio and television stations, direct mail, or neighborhood publications and community fundraisers.

Traditional ad channels can be effective depending on the nature of your business, but they have some definite limitations. First, it's difficult to know exactly how many people are able to view the ads. Second, it's hard to know that the audience includes the type of people who would even be interested in your products or services in the first place.

Now that Facebook's user base has expanded to include people from virtually every demographic group—young or old, urban or country, male or female—you know your target can be reached with a Facebook ad. People of all ages, backgrounds and interests are using the site to connect with their friends and family. And many of them are heavy Facebook users, spending time on the site on a regular basis, sometimes every day.

While the number of people that your ad will reach is determined mostly by your budget, knowing that so many different types of consumers use the site virtually guarantees you'll be able reach your ideal potential customers, which brings us to our next point.

Facebook Ads can be highly targeted. After knowing that your ad will be seen, the next most important aspect to any successful ad campaign is the ability to get it in front of your "target demographic," the type of consumer most likely to purchase what you're offering.

Facebook's paid ad platform's process has a step called "Choose Your Audience" that allows you to target users who fit an ideal set of traits. This allows you to target your ad toward users located in a certain geographical area, members of a certain age group, those that have specific interests, and those with many other personal attributes. This precise targeting is possible because Facebook users have volunteered these personal characteristics, enabling marketers like you to reach exactly who you want to reach.

For example, imagine that you're running a small local lawn care business. You would be able to create an ad campaign that shows up for any, or all of, the traits listed below:

- Users who are aged 27 and up, who are most likely to own or rent their own homes with lawns
- Users who live in your area code and surrounding areas. This ensures you don't waste money showing your ad to people who live outside your service area
- Users who've recently moved into your area, and probably haven't yet hired a local lawn service or landscaper

This ability to target individuals that fit certain criteria ensures that you only pay to show your ad to Facebook users who are likely to buy. The cost of your campaign will increase depending on how "targeted" it is, but it's a very worthwhile trade off knowing that your ad budget will be spent efficiently.

Because Facebook's ad platform is readily adjustable and responsive, you can create time-sensitive targeted campaigns that reach users with upcoming birthdays. You can tie your ad to upcoming holidays or a major sporting event, enabling you to reach users who might be shopping for related gifts or services.

For example, imagine you sell custom-made jewelry online. In just a few minutes, you can create an ad targeting college students right before Mother's Day, offering a welcome solution for those searching for a special gift. The targeting options are vast, and we'll cover this step in more detail later in this chapter.

Facebook ads complement your other marketing efforts. For a variety of reasons, Facebook ads can directly enhance all of your other online marketing efforts. On their own, Facebook ads can be used to raise general awareness for your business and generate sales, but also maximize the return on investment (ROI) for your other online efforts, on Facebook and beyond.

For example, consider a typical Facebook campaign, which funnels visitors to your business Page (or as they're now known, "timeline"). When visitors Like your Page as a result of your ad, the friends of those users will see the news in their feed, too. This not only adds to your fan count, giving you added credibility, but adds a social, viral momentum to your campaign.

Facebook's timeline can also be fully integrated with your own website, blog or other social networking accounts like Twitter. For example, if you wish, you can automatically feed your Facebook timeline with your Twitter updates. Alternatively, if you have an outside website, blog, Etsy account, or other online store, you can link your ad directly to these destinations. We'll examine the pros and cons of each approach later in this chapter.

The effectiveness of Facebook ad campaigns is highly measurable. One of the most impressive and useful features Facebook provides businesses is the fact that it allows you to see real-time statistics regarding the effectiveness and overall reach of your paid ad campaigns. This is probably its most notable difference from traditional offline advertising platforms, and if used correctly, can help even the most novice marketer create a very effective and mature ad strategy.

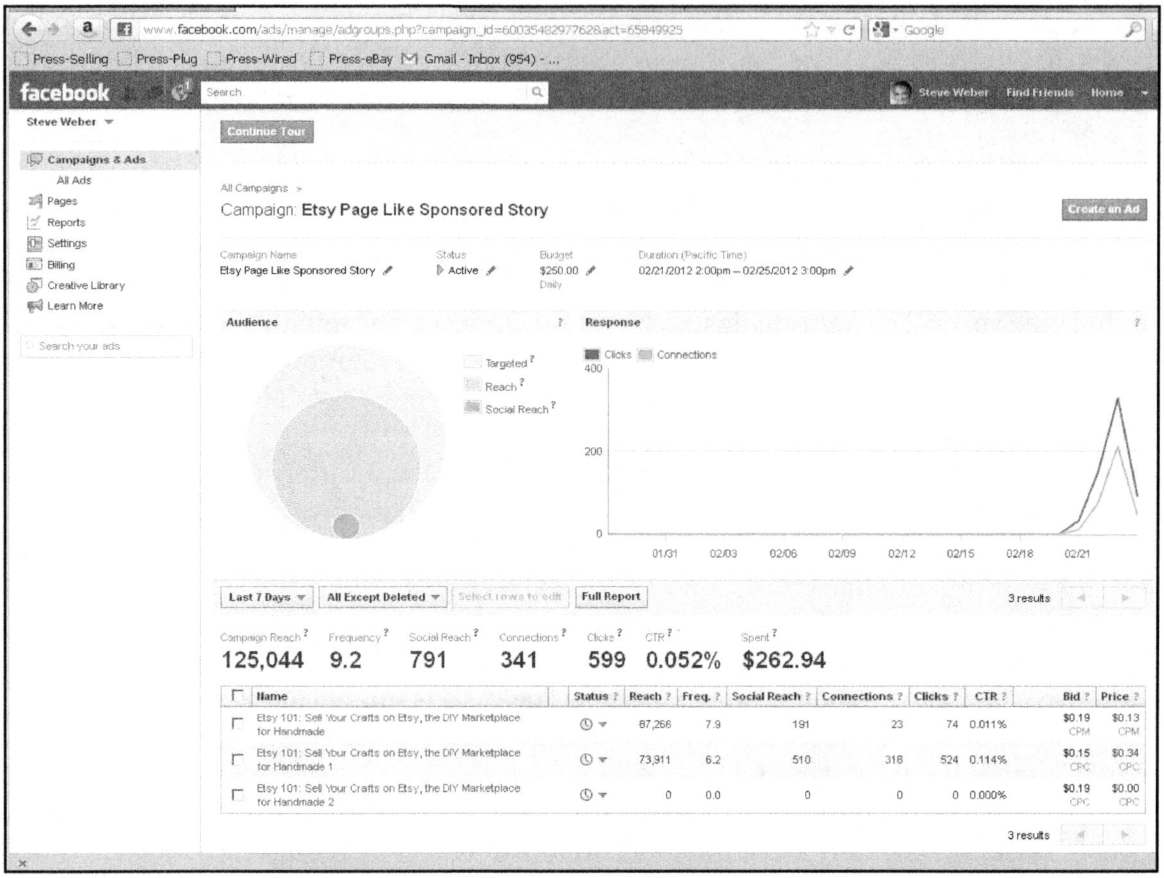

For each of your campaigns, Facebook tracks a number of statistics that will help you understand exactly how many people are clicking on or seeing your ads, as well as how they are interacting with them. These stats are constantly being updated as these interactions occur, and they include things like your click-through rate (CTR), total impressions (number of times your ad appears to a Facebook user), and how many "clicks" your ad has generated.

Combined with the "Insights" tool, which is available to any business with a Facebook page (even if you choose not to pay for ads), this stat tracking allows you to keep a close eye on your time and cash investment into all of your Facebook marketing endeavors. By keeping an astute watch on how your stats are developing over time, and making note of what does and doesn't work, you can make constant alterations to your strategy that will help you make the most out of everything you do on the site.

Facebook ad campaigns aren't cheap, but they are affordable and very scalable. For small businesses, one of the best aspects of paid Facebook marketing is that you decide exactly how much you want to pay for ads. You can determine how much, or little, you want to spend every day for a campaign, or how much you want to invest over its lifetime. Unlike traditional forms of paid advertising, there are no set rates or minimums imposed on any given campaign. Of course, the more you're willing to spend, the more impressions and clicks you'll get.

This makes Facebook ads an extremely attractive option to get your paid advertising presence off the ground as you expand your customer base. Once you begin seeing a return on your ad campaign, you can then reinvest the cash you earn.

Coupled with the tracking and analysis features of Facebook's ad campaign platform, you can start your paid advertising with very minimal risk, and take a trial-and-error approach to campaign creation. If you start with a small campaign, and it doesn't work well for any reason, you can pause or end it, return to the proverbial drawing board, and try again.

Now you know the unique benefits that paid Facebook ads have over other forms of paid advertising. You'll learn even faster by actually getting your feet wet and trying a real campaign.

Starting your first campaign

The basics: Before we jump into a step-by-step example of how to create your first ad's content, get it posted, and analyze the results, we're going to take a quick look at the fundamental basics of the Facebook ad platform. These next few steps will be very basic but cover the necessary square-one steps of getting your first campaign up and running.

What is a Facebook Ad? Sure, we've talked plenty about the ideas, benefits and theory behind paid Facebook ads, but where are they located on the site? What do they consist of?

Facebook ads appear in the sidebar on the right of the user's screen, in between the main content and mini-feed/chat box. This location is ideal, as most user interaction with the site happens in this area. They're also on nearly every page while users surf Facebook, with the exception of the "help" and ad platform sections of the site. Typically, there will be multiple ads, at least three or four per page, placed vertically down the side of the page.

There are two types of ads for you to choose from: "Ads" and "Sponsored Stories." Both have the same fundamental elements—an image, a headline and some text at the bottom. The image and headline are designed to draw attention, and the text usually urges the reader to take some action, such as visiting a Web page or "liking" your page.

As a part of the text area, you can include links out to your own external website, and the ubiquitous Facebook Like button appears (as long as the ad is linked to your business's timeline). If a user's friends have already Liked your post or business, their names will automatically appear as part of your ad like this screen shot here. For example, consider this ad for Target appearing at the top of my Facebook profile. It automatically points out which of my friends Like Target, helping to catch my eye and involve me with the ad.

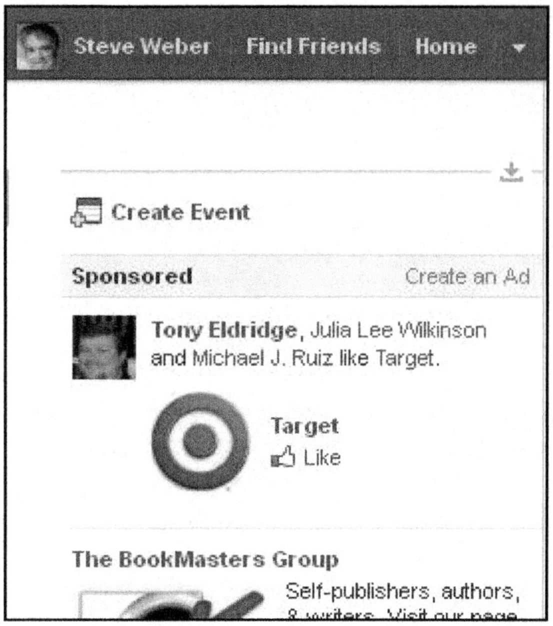

The difference between Standard Ads and Sponsored Stories: The two types of ads that Facebook currently offers share a very similar posting process and aesthetic, but also have different aims. For the purposes of this book, we'll be breaking them down into these two distinct categories: standard ads and sponsored stories.

Standard Ads

Here are two standard ads as they appear stacked in the right sidebar. Each has the same three elements: An image, a headline and text. And they're linked to a webpage or Facebook page describing the product and a special offer.

The standard ad was, until very recently, the only type of ad that was available for purchase on Facebook. Even though they might seem simplistic in nature, standard ads give you much more creative freedom than sponsored story ads do.

Due to the open-ended nature of what you can display to users with standard ads, they are ideal for several different purposes, and should make up a majority of your paid Facebook marketing efforts. They make it possible to run Facebook-related special offers, use fun and creative efforts to attract clicks, or convey a very specific message to your potential customers. This versatility is what makes the standard ad the primary choice when running a paid ad on Facebook.

Sponsored Story Ads

To illustrate a sponsored story ad, let's take a look at the Target ad we viewed earlier.

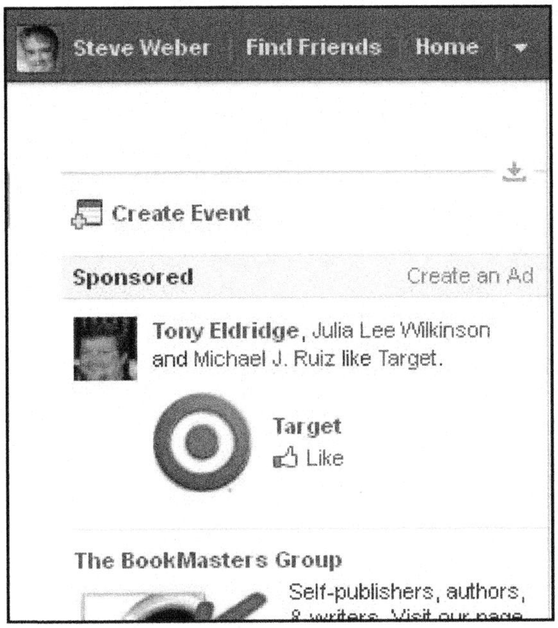

Sponsored story ads are a relatively new addition to the Facebook ad platform, and while not as versatile as standard ads, they have a definite purpose. Instead of giving you the freedom to craft the aesthetic of your ad by providing the image and text, they are designed to highlight a specific piece of content that you have already uploaded to your business's timeline. The ad's content is "auto-created" for you, and your only choices will be your targeting selections and payment options.

Don't discount sponsored stories as merely a "dumbed-down" version of a standard ad, for there is a notable difference. Sponsored stories highlight your business and your message by showing which friends of a user have already liked, interacted with, or visited your business through Facebook's "check-in" feature.

The information in this type of ad appears much differently than it does in a standard ad. Instead of just highlighting your business, the ad will show a picture of one of the viewer's friends who has already interacted with the content you chose to create the ad around. You can also choose to have the ad highlight when a viewer's friends Like your page or check-in to your business's location. All of the names of the user's other friends who have also interacted with your business will appear, too, as well as the Like button.

The connection with friends enhances your credibility and makes your ad infinitely more interesting to viewers. Although this content also appears (organically with no paid advertising required) in the "feed" section when a friend visits the site, this exposure is fleeting, and it is quickly buried by other activity. By paying for a sponsored story ad, you can prolong this valuable exposure. Your target audience is more likely to take action and click on these ads because a personal connection implies that a friend or relative is actually recommending your business.

So even though sponsored stories are computer-generated "word of mouth," circumstances can limit their effectiveness. For example, when you're first building your business's Facebook presence, sponsored stories won't be effective because they're only shown to users whose friends have already interacted with your business. This severely limits the visibility of your ad. Also, with limited control over what information is displayed in sponsored stories, you are limited in the kind of message to convey. But, if you already have an established timeline for your business, and have a substantial following, it can be a great way to raise exposure and awareness for your business.

Logging into the Ad Manager

The first step in getting your first campaign underway is logging into Facebook's ad system.

There are numerous ways to get into the ad platform section of Facebook, though the easiest is to simply go to Facebook's homepage, and scroll down to the bottom. There, you'll find a list of links on the horizontal navigation bar. The first link is "About" and the second is "Advertising." Click on the advertising link to visit Facebook's Ad Center.

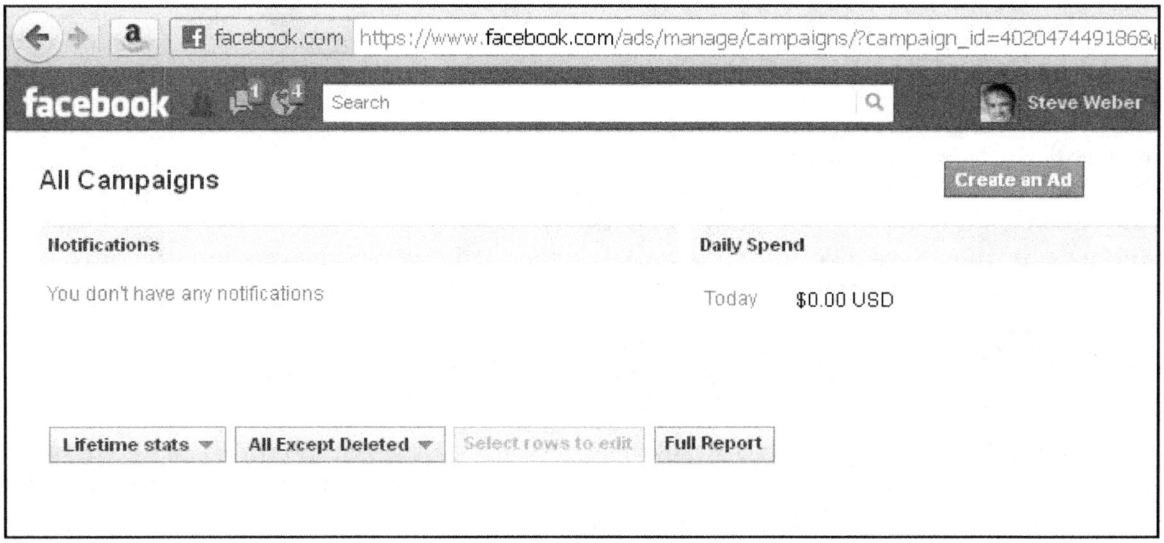

Alternatively, you can also type www.Facebook.com/ads into your browser's address bar to reach the ad creation page. Also, to visit the ad platform, you must be logged into your personal Facebook profile, not your business page.

On the home page of Facebook's ad section, you'll see a link to the ad campaign management interface and a green "Create an Ad" button on the right.

Let's jump right in with a step-by-step walkthrough of posting your first ad. If you're reading this book on your computer or in front of it, go ahead and click that green create an ad button in the top right corner of the advertising home page now. Don't worry about making a mistake, you can revise or delete the ad if necessary.

The ad creation process

Facebook's ad creation tool guides you through all the steps required to post an ad. However, the site won't explain how to craft an effective ad that will provide the maximum return for your business. That's exactly what this section of the book is about.

Also, remember that as you go through the ad creation process, a preview of your ad will appear on the right-hand side of your screen and change as you make your choices. This is invaluable, as it will allow you to play around with the different options without committing to anything and give you an accurate depiction of what your ad will look like to viewers. You'll also see the number of potential viewers your ad will have (your campaign's potential "reach") as you go along. This number doesn't mean you'll get that many views, as that's determined by your budget, but it does reflect the maximum number of different people that could theoretically see your ad.

Setting up your Ad or Sponsored Story

These next few pages will teach you exactly how to approach each step of the process to create an ad that falls under the platform's "Set up your ad or Sponsored Story" section.

After clicking the "Create an Ad" button, you'll arrive here, at the Ad Creation page:

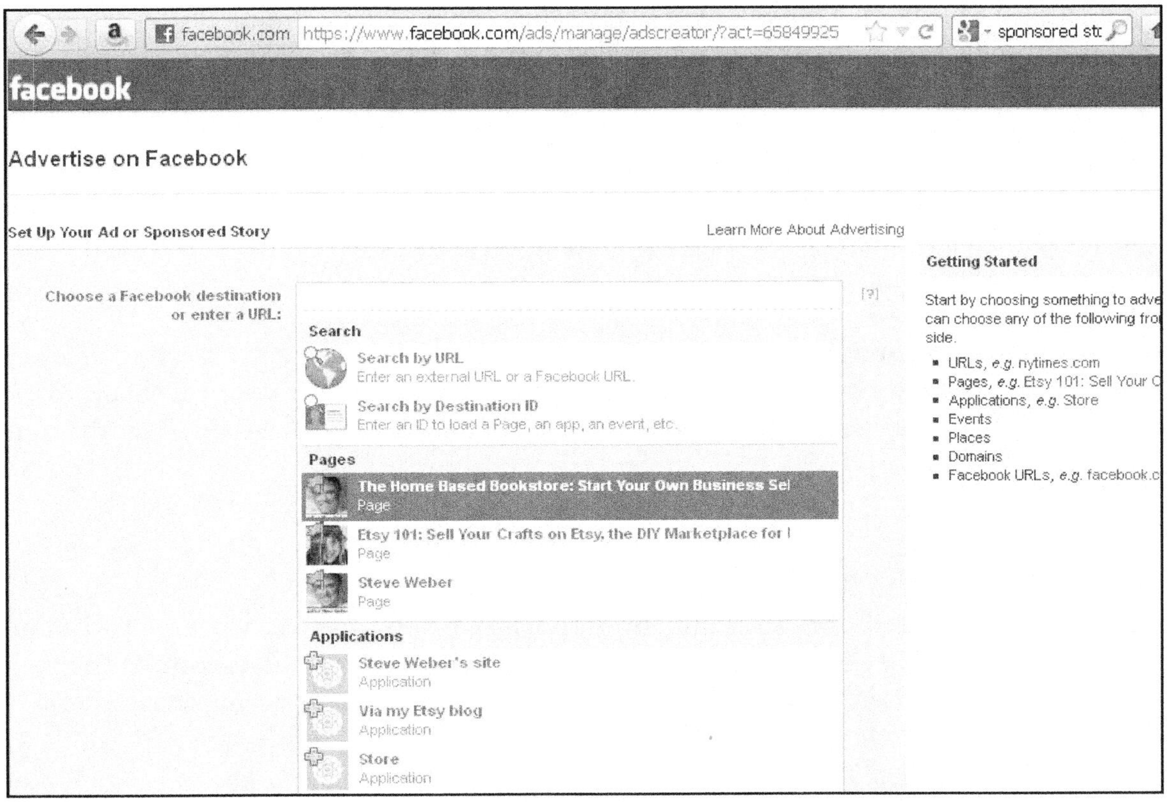

Choosing your ad's "Facebook Destination or Outside URL": The first space in this form is a blank line labeled "Choose a Facebook destination or enter a URL." Your selection at this step will determine the other choices that you're given later on in the process.

To choose your destination, you'll see a drop-down list of options that consists of your existing Facebook Pages, or you can enter the URL of an outside website. Depending on the type of ad you want to create (standard ad or sponsored story), you'll approach this in different ways.

To create a Standard Ad

If you want to create a standard ad (probably the best choice if this is your first ad), you have a few different options:

Choose your business's timeline or "place" page. By selecting one of your business's pages on Facebook, any user that clicks on your ad will be forwarded to that page. This is useful if you're trying to increase the Like count on your page and expose viewers to other content that you've posted on the site. Combined with a strategic collection of posted content, this can be a very effective ad. More Likes gives you a higher level of perceived credibility, which enhances trust and increase the chances that the visitor will engage with your business.

Enter a URL (web address) to an outside web page such as www.mysite.com. If you choose to enter an outside URL, users will be transferred from Facebook to your external site. The page will open in a new tab in the user's browser, so their Facebook session isn't interrupted.

If you want to promote your business in general, it's best to link out to the most informational content that you've created for your business. This will allow users who click on the ad to gain the most knowledge about your products or services, and it provides the best chance to help potential customers learn what you're all about. An example of this might be a landing page or welcome video.

Alternatively, you might want to use your ad to attract direct sales—by advertising a specific promotion, product or service package at your external URL. While it's likely this won't give you the best chance of getting a user to Like your business or build brand awareness, this is a good alternative if you're running a holiday-driven sales campaign.

Have a good publicity campaign going. Let's imagine your business recently received an award, was written up in the newspaper, or mentioned on a popular blog. You might use your Facebook ad to forward readers to the flattering coverage. While you might not get many direct sales or Likes, this can enhance your brand and credibility.

To create a Sponsored Story Ad

If you want to create a sponsored story ad (again, this is advisable only after you've developed a fan base), your "destination" options are limited to your business's Facebook page and its content. Why? Sponsored stories highlight the interactions that the viewer's friends have had with your business on Facebook itself.

Unlike a standard ad, your only choice for the destination of a sponsored story is your business Page. Ultimately, the ad can either direct the viewer to your general timeline, a specific piece of content on it, or an event page of your choosing. In the next step of the ad-creation process, you'll select exactly what the ad will highlight.

Choose "What You Want to Promote": In this example, we're promoting a business page. In the following illustration, I've selected my business page and arrived at this screen:

Note: If you chose an outside URL as your ad's destination, you'll be bypassing this step and you'll immediately be asked to start creating the content that will make up your ad. It's still a good idea to read this section of the book though, for future reference.

At this stage, we've selected the business Page being promoted, and we're asked, "What do you want to promote?" This is one of the most straightforward and simple steps of the process of creating an ad, and it will look exactly the same whether you want to create a standard ad or Sponsored Story.

Your choices here are the name of your business or "a specific post" on your business Page. If you want to promote your Page in general, click on the button next to just your business's name. This is the option you'll select if your main goal is to generate Likes on your page or raise awareness of your brand.

If you have a specific piece of content or an event that you'd like to promote, you'll want to select the "a specific post on ..." option. Once you've done this, you'll see a drop down menu appear with a list of the posts on your page. If you want to promote an event, make sure it is selected. If you want to highlight a piece of content on your time line, indicate which one.

If you click the button for "A specific post," a checkbox will appear with an option to "always promote my most recent post." Selecting this updates your ad with your newest Facebook content each time you post to your timeline. Usually this isn't a good choice because it limits the control and efficiency of your ad. Don't use this option unless you have a logical and defined reason to do so.

If you decide to promote a specific post, you'll also notice that you are given the option to add URL tracking tags to your ad. This is an advanced feature that requires a little web programming knowledge, and it won't actually change the effectiveness of your ad. Its purpose is to allow you to differentiate (or track) the traffic you get from the ad from the organic traffic your post generates (news feed clicks, clicks generated from "surfing", etc.). While it's a nice feature to have, it's usually unnecessary.

Promoting an Event on Facebook

If you're an artist, venue or organization using Facebook to generate awareness and participation in an event described on your Page, you can choose to promote it during this step. Although this approach has a limited application, it can be very powerful when combined with a set of effective "targeting" choices.

Advertising an event enables you to place a listing for the event before a set of Facebook users that reside within a certain distance of the event site. Since people are often interacting with local friends on Facebook, they can pass along word of the event after viewing your ad. Combined with the sponsored story option, users will even be informed of which friends have already RSVP'd. Imagine what that could do to your attendance numbers!

The 'People will see' selection

If you've chosen to promote your business, place page, or an event (instead of an outside URL), you'll arrive at the page below. Here, we'll specify what "People will see" after clicking on the ad. You'll have two or three choices, such as "A new ad" about your company, "Stories about their friends liking" your company or event post, or "Stories about their friends checking in to your place." You'll only see the last option if you're a brick-and-mortar establishment.

Your selection here is the final choice that will determine whether or not you post a standard ad or sponsored story ad. The rule of thumb here is that if you click the button next to an option that starts with the word "story," you'll be posting a sponsored story (simple enough, right?). Any other choice will create a standard ad that promotes your business in general. Once you've done this, you'll be ready to move on—you'll either pick your targeting options or create the custom content of your ad, depending on the type of ad you want.

Crafting the content of your ad

The decisions you make regarding the content in your ad are a critical part of the ad-creation process. Because of the creative freedom allowed here, it's where a lot of mistakes are made. When creating a standard ad that links to an outside URL or your business's timeline, the possibilities for mistakes are vast.

With a sponsored story ad or one that highlights a specific post from your timeline, you're much more limited in what you can do. In fact, you'll be able to skip this step entirely and move directly on to the "Choose your Audience" phase of the ad creation process. Facebook will have already auto-generated your content, no alterations are possible.

The process for uploading and writing your ad's text (or ad "copy" as it's known in advertising lingo) is very streamlined. Now, how will you decide what to say? Keep reading.

Art and Copy: the creative side of the advertising world

When you're creating a standard ad on Facebook, you're given a varying amount of freedom regarding what you can input, depending on whether your ad's destination is an outside URL or your business's timeline or place page. An ad linking out to an outside URL will allow you to change the headline, body copy and image of the ad. An ad that sends viewers to your Facebook page forces you to use your page's name as the headline, but you're still able to choose your own image and body text.

There are literally millions of ways to handle the creative part of an ad. That's why expert graphic artists and copywriters are some of the highest paid workers in marketing. We'll discuss exactly how to approach the creative side of your ad, but first we'll cover a few art and copy basics.

Facebook Ad copy and image details

Copy/text: Writing the copy/text for a Facebook ad might seem extremely easy on the surface. Limited space allows you only 25 characters for your headline and 90 for the body text. So you don't have to write much, but you need to make what you write count. Whenever you write copy for a Facebook ad, be sure to get straight to the point. Prune any "fluff" or unnecessary words. Make it clear what you want to reader to do by using verbs: Save money. Get it free. Read more.

Remember that Facebook is committed to being a family-friendly place. No salty language; keep things tasteful. If your branding is a bit controversial, some tongue-in-cheek humor is okay, but err on the side of caution. Otherwise your ad might be flagged for removal from the site. Repeated offenses can result in your being banned from posting ads.

Images: The image dimensions for a Facebook ad are 110 pixels by 80 pixels. That's pretty small, so select or create an image that doesn't have a great deal of fine detail, which will get lost. Facebook will automatically scale your image to its proportions when you upload it, so if you use a much larger image, you'll lose a whole lot of quality. The key is to find or make an image close to the recommended size that doesn't have a lot of fine detail.

One of the biggest issues when choosing an image for your ads is avoiding copyright infringement. If you didn't create the image, be sure you have permission to use it. You can search for suitable images at a variety of marketplaces online, such as BigStockPhoto.com, iStockPhoto.com, and www.sxc.hu. The use of some photos requires you to pay a licensing fee which can range from a few dollars to many, while others are free. Be sure to read the licensing terms.

Just as with the ad copy you use, it's very important to select an appropriate, tasteful image for your ad. Facebook is even more selective with the images it allows in ads than the text. They say "sex sells," but not on Facebook. Unless there is a reason for a woman in a bikini in your ad (for instance, if you're selling bikinis), Facebook won't allow it. That doesn't mean you can't use an image of an attractive female to draw eyeballs, but they will allow no hint of nudity.

Write effective ad copy

Writing copy is an art. It's easy to do, but tough to master. It takes much practice, and most people must try several times, revising and polishing, before they find something suitable. It's worth the effort. Good copy makes ads work. Here are a few good tips for writing ad copy:

- **Speak to your customer.** Whenever you write copy, craft it in a way so that those you hope to reach will respond to it. For example, if you're selling your product to college students, be upbeat and fun. If you are selling a self-help product to help people get over a stressful situation, be empathetic and understanding. Imagine your typical customers and write your copy as if you're speaking directly to them, face-to-face. Write exactly how you'd speak to them in person.

- **No hard sell.** Direct sales are hard to generate on Facebook because most people use it for socializing, not shopping. Users rarely respond to ads that trumpet, "Get 50 percent off any order." The reader probably doesn't know anything about you or your product yet, so any mention of a "discount" isn't going to spark their interest. It just makes their eyes glaze over.

The best way to sell something is to use your ad as an introduction. Tell the customer who and what you are, then let them create their own thoughts based around your product or service. If you've been using your timeline or website effectively, they'll take the direction.

- **Add value.** The best way to make an ad enticing is to offer something free, perhaps a free report or video. If you have informative blog articles, videos or other content out on the web, highlight it. Here's an example:

Imagine you operate a custom jewelry business. You might post an article on your blog or timeline revealing the five must-have necklaces for this summer. This is the kind of content Facebook users will enjoy passing along to their friends, and it will highlight your products in a subtle way. Here, your ad will refer to your article, not directly to your product. A good headline might be, "Keep Your Neck Cool..." and for the body, "this summer with these 5 types of trendy necklaces. Click to see the hottest styles."

This is a good ad because it's about the target customer, not your business. Instead of selling directly, it offers something of value—style advice and fun ideas. Those who click on the ad will be funneled to your blog or website to view your article. Then, the task is to convert the visitor into a paying customer.

Three specific Facebook Ad copy strategies

1. To raise awareness of your business or brand: Raising awareness on Facebook means generating Likes, getting your business's name out there, and keeping your content appearing in users' news feeds. Here, it's prudent to send viewers to your timeline or Page for one of your first ads. So, during Facebook's ad creation "What people will see" step, select your business's timeline or place page and "a new ad for your business." Remember with this strategy your ad headline must be your Page name.

To write copy for this type of ad, take an honest approach and highlight the benefit that your business offers customers and avoid the hard sell. Try to pique the viewer's interest by telling them what you can do for them or what you've already done for your existing customers. If you have a company mission statement, this would be a great piece of text to refer to. Here are a few examples:

- **Lawn care/landscaping business** - Sore back? Let us take care of backbreaking, sweaty yard work for you.
- **Handmade jewelry business** - Show that you're a discerning woman of the world with unique, affordable, yet elegant accessories.
- **Coffee shop** - Meet friends and get your caffeine fix. Free refills and Wi-Fi in a smoke-free environment.

2. To highlight an outside piece of content. This strategy is very much like the "add value with copy" point we made in the previous section. The aim is to build relationships with customers by referring them to your online marketing materials away from Facebook. If you have blog posts relating to your industry, PR pieces on the web, or video content, use it here.

You'll be using an outside URL as your ad's destination, so you'll need to create a headline as well as body text. The best option here is to refer to something other than your business, in order to highlight the value of the content and generate the click. Here's how you would do that:

- **Lawn care/landscaping** - Headline: "Landscaping Is an Art" Body text: "Check out these 5 lawns guaranteed to make your neighbors green." Link to a blog piece with photos of your best work.
- **Handmade quilts** - Headline: "Keep Toasty This Winter" Body text: "With these made-to-order masterpieces. Click now for your heirloom." Link to your online catalog or photos of samples.
- **Pizza parlor/delivery service** - Headline: "Hungry for Pizza?" Body text: "Print coupons for half-price pies with free drinks and delivery, good for the rest of the month." The ad links to your webpage displaying the coupons (perhaps for new customers only).

3. To generate direct sales. If you want your ad to generate some direct sales, your ad needs to link out to your website's sale page. It's important to offer some sort of discount code or incentive, perhaps time-sensitive or holiday-focused. There are many ads for "sales," so to stand out among competitors, you'll need to offer something special.

The key to writing a good sales ad is to craft a unique approach, as opposed to a straight offer like "order now, 25 percent off your order." You don't have much space, so it's a challenge. Be certain you can handle any spike in demand. Here are a few examples of how to run a "direct sales" type of ad:

- **Lawn care/landscaping.** Headline: "Pro Landscaping, Great Rates" Body text: "It's hot outside, but not as hot as this deal. Take 50% off your first mow by mentioning this ad."
- **Handmade soap** - Headline: "Surprise for Mother's Day?" Body text: "Buy heavenly soap for her, get one free for yourself. Click here to order.
- **Bakery** - Headline: "Your Birthday Present From Us" Body Text: "Custom birthday cakes and cupcakes, delivered fresh from $19.95." You've targeted likely cake buyers—females aged 25 to 55 in your area with approaching birthdays.

Picking the right image

After you've determined the approach you'll take with your ad's text, you'll need the perfect image to complement it. Your goal is to find an eye-catching illustration that reinforces the idea of your ad. Facebook pages are filled with clutter, so your small ad image has a lot of work to do to attract attention.

If you have some design skills or know someone who does, commissioning or making your own image is an option. You're only limited by your creativity, but here are a few very solid guidelines to follow when choosing your image:

Wacky and funny - If you can find an image that relates to the text in your ad but is a bit ridiculous, it's probably a pretty good one. These types of images usually stand out well and don't come off as just another boring advertisement.

Cute can be great too - If your business or ad uses an emotional approach to its sell, using an image with some "cute" in it can be great. Small children and animals fit this profile extremely well.

Pictures of women are always a good bet - If there's one thing marketing experts agree on, it's that ads featuring images of attractive women are usually more effective than those featuring men, no matter who your target is. Psychologists claim that women will put themselves in the shoes of the woman in the ad, and men usually enjoy looking at women.

Use a logo for branding/consumer awareness - If you're making an ad that refers individuals to your timeline in general, it's best to simply use your logo. You want people to recognize your brand and this is how it's done.

Choose Your Audience step

Once you've settled on your ad's art and copy, the next step in Facebook's ad-creation procedure is "Choose your Audience." It's probably the most important step in the process, with the creative portion coming in at a close second. However, once you understand the correct approach, choosing your audience is a very logical and intuitive task. By now you've learned how to choose the type of ad you should post to accomplish different goals. Picking your targets will take the work you've done there, and make sure that your ad gets in front of the right viewers.

The more highly targeted your ad, the more it will likely cost because of increased competition. However, this is a great trade-off because it ensures that your ad will be as effective as possible. It's much better to invest a little more in something that will get in front of your ideal customer, as opposed to skimping to show your ad to folks who aren't interested. Niches and micro-niches are where you'll find your best customers.

If you chose to create a sponsored story, your ad will automatically target only the friends of users who've already Liked or interacted with your timeline or place Page. If you chose to create a standard ad, your potential audience is anyone who has a Facebook profile. Regardless of which type of ad you created, you'll still be able to further define the users that will be able to see your ad.

Here is how you should approach each choice in the "choose your audience" section of the ad creation tool:

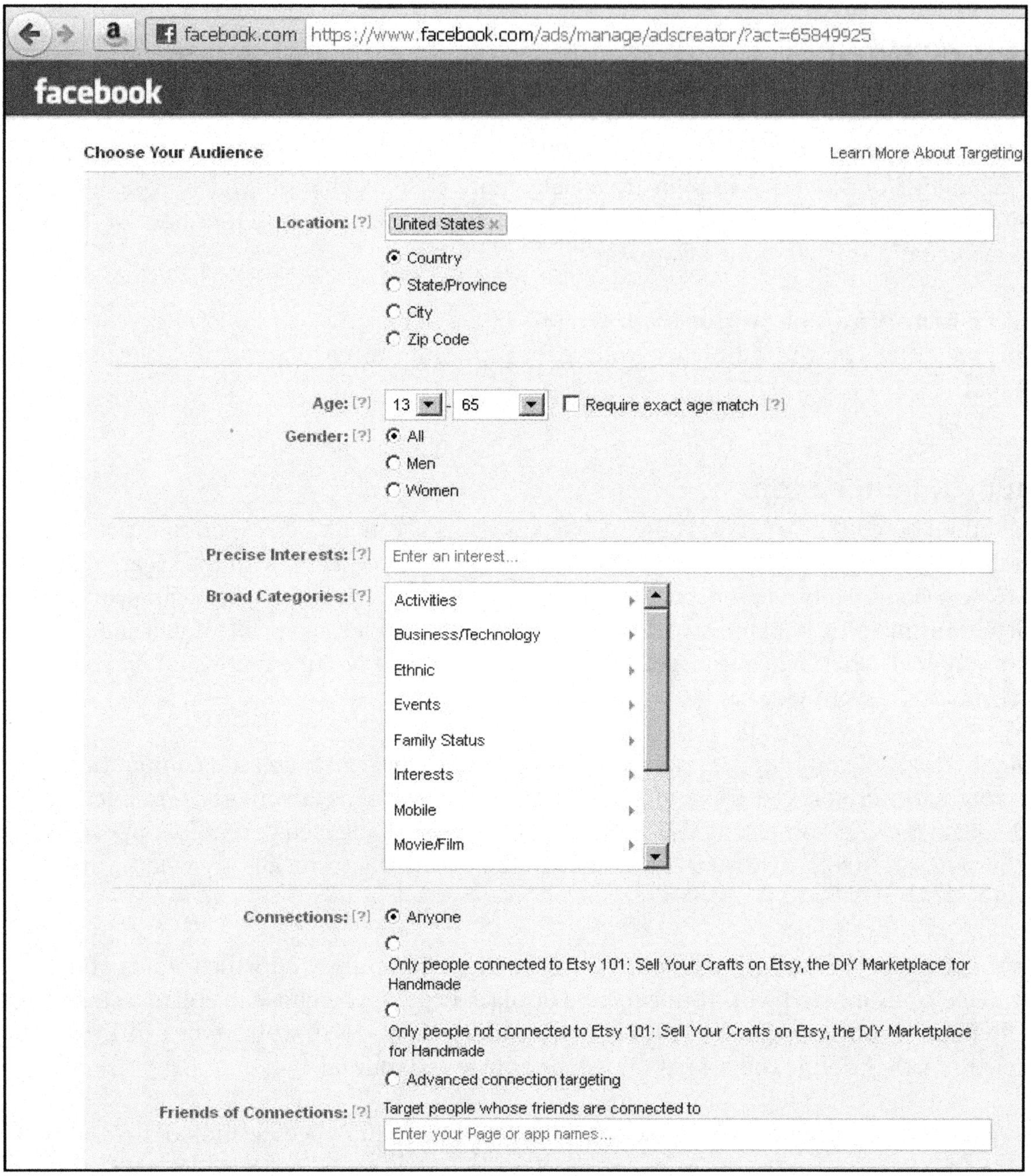

Location

The location choices determine what geographical area your ad will appear in. Narrow it down by selecting only the area that your business serves. It ensures that your ad will only display for users that you can actually sell to.

If you operate a brick-and-mortar establishment, your best bet is to choose either the city or zip code option and type in the areas closest to you. It's recommended that you don't stray too far away from your business, as it's unlikely that viewers farther than 25 miles away will travel to visit a typical business. If you operate a pizza delivery service in New Jersey, you don't want to waste your money advertising to people in California.

If your establishment draws customers from a larger region, then expand your geographic targeting. If you operate a business that ships nationally, you'll want to select users in your specific country. If you ship internationally, you might want to skip inputting anything here during this step, as it will allow you to reach Facebook users on a global scale. Remember the potential language barriers, though. If your business only operates in English, showing your ad in Russia will be less effective. (In addition to targeting users by geographic boundaries, you can select some language restrictions later in the "targeting" phase.)

Age and sex

Age and sex targeting can get a bit tricky, as making the proper choices is entirely dependent on your product, service and your ad's content and strategy. For most ads, begin by asking, who is my typical customer? In other words, keep your target demographic in mind, and choose accordingly.

If your ad is designed to speak directly to a specific type of person—new mothers, softball players, pottery collectors, for example—you'd want to pick the age and sex that would most likely include these folks.

Interests

The "interests" section is the most difficult part of the Choose Your Audience step, and for good reason. It's the only one that's entirely open-ended, allowing you to enter your original wording. The options that you choose here will tell Facebook to scan the information on user's profiles, and show your ad only to those who have expressed an interest in the options you choose.

The fields available to you here are "broad interests" (such as "reading" or "books") and "precise interests" (such as "thrillers" or "comedies"). You may target a combination of both broad and precise interests. With precise targeting, you can begin to type in your own ideas, and as you type, Facebook will suggest options as you go along. With broad targeting, you'll scan a menu of predefined choices. You'll notice that as you make these choices, the number of individuals that exhibit your selected set of traits is displayed. The more narrow your targeting, the smaller the available population will be, but the more likely they'll be interested in your ad.

Choose the interests that are most closely related to your product or service, or that your target demographic will identify with. Remember, you can also target people with upcoming life events or certain background traits as well—like upcoming birthdays, recent moves, or members of certain ethnic groups.

One available technique is to "piggyback" onto a large company or brand, and select individuals who've expressed interests in that product. For example, if you operate a local microbrewery, you might target folks who've expressed interest in "beer making" or "brewing." Perhaps you'd like to target fans of related brands like "Heineken."

Connections

The "Connections" feature enables you to show your ad or sponsored story only to members with a connection to your Page, app or event. If you'd like to show the ad to people who Like your Page, select the option under "Advanced Connections Targeting."

Advanced targeting options

The advanced targeting options are extremely contextual and will only apply to very specific types of products. You should be able to identify if your product would benefit by one of these options by now, but here are a few common examples of when they should be used:

- You offer an educational product that is only in specific languages.
- You offer a product that is only for singles or married folks.
- You're a company that serves employees of a large company with a local office (uniform company, restaurant close by an office building, etc.).
- You offer a product relevant only to students of a certain level.

Examples of effective targeting

Here are a few examples of some options that different types of businesses might choose:

A handmade jewelry business that ships nationally

- Women 16 and up
- Those interested in fashion or accessories
- Those who have a birthday coming up (might be looking for suggestions for their gift-giving friends and family)
- Those interested in competing brands (piggybacking)
- Those who live in your country

Valentine's Day direct sales promotion

- Men aged 16 and up
- Those who are in a relationship, engaged or married
- Those who live in your country

A local café

- Men and women 18 and up
- Interested in coffee
- Fans of large national coffee houses
- Interested in reading or writing (these activities are common for coffee houses)
- Live relatively close to your location

Advertising a business-informational product with worldwide appeal

- Men and women aged 22 and up
- Interested in entrepreneurship or business
- List their profession as small business owner
- Speak the language that your product is in
- Come from any location (leave location options blank)

Paying for, scheduling, and monitoring your ad

Once you've targeted your ad, you're nearly ready to post your first ad. You just need to select your payment structure and schedule. You'll be billed daily, up to the maximum amount you've indicated.

By now, you should have a very accurate depiction of what your ad will look like on the right of your screen, as well as a clear number of how many different people your ad could reach. The number that it will actually reach, however, is completely determined by your budget. The figure given only reflects the maximum number.

Objectives

CPC Versus CPM: The first option you'll see during this process is "Objective." It's a small drop down field that has two options: "Like my page" and "Click my ad or Sponsored Story." What you're actually choosing here is whether to pay for cost-per-click (CPC) or cost-per-thousand impressions (CPM).

CPM – "Those likely to like your ad": CPM or cost-per-thousand impressions means you'll pay a certain rate for every 1,000 times your ad is displayed on a Facebook user's screen. This option is best chosen if you're trying to spread your branding and consumer awareness, as more people will see it than with CPC. Obviously, the more you pay, the more impressions you'll get. If you are running an ad that promotes your page or business in general, or are working on a very small budget, this is likely the choice for you.

CPC – "Those likely to click your ad or Sponsored Story": With CPC, you'll pay each time a Facebook user clicks on your ad or sponsored story. This is ideal if you're trying to guide users to an outside URL for a direct sales campaign, for example, or to funnel traffic to a certain page. With CPC, you're required to "bid" for each click. Facebook will suggest a range for your bid, and this is because the ad platform works much like an auction. Higher bids appear more frequently, and lower bids are shown less often.

Which is better for your ad, CPC or CPM? Well, it all depends on your objective, whether it's branding or selling. CPM usually provides more exposure for each ad dollar spent, which can help your brand stick in the minds of your target audience. But for direct sales, you'll be better served with CPC. You'll probably pay more and your ad will be seen fewer times, but those who click on it will generally be more interested and likely to buy.

Setting your budget, payment method, and schedule

Next you'll select your country's currency, the country you're located in, your time zone, and campaign name. The location/currency options are for billing purposes, and aren't related to your ad performance. The campaign name is for your internal campaign analysis use only.

You may choose to set a daily budget for your ad or a lifetime budget. The safest method is to set a daily budget and monitor ad performance every day. If you set a daily budget and performance is unsatisfactory, you may pause or cancel the ad at any time. With a lifetime budget, canceling an ad is a bit more complicated. Also, the performance of any ad will deteriorate over time after it has had significant exposure among the target audience—a phenomenon known as "ad fatigue."

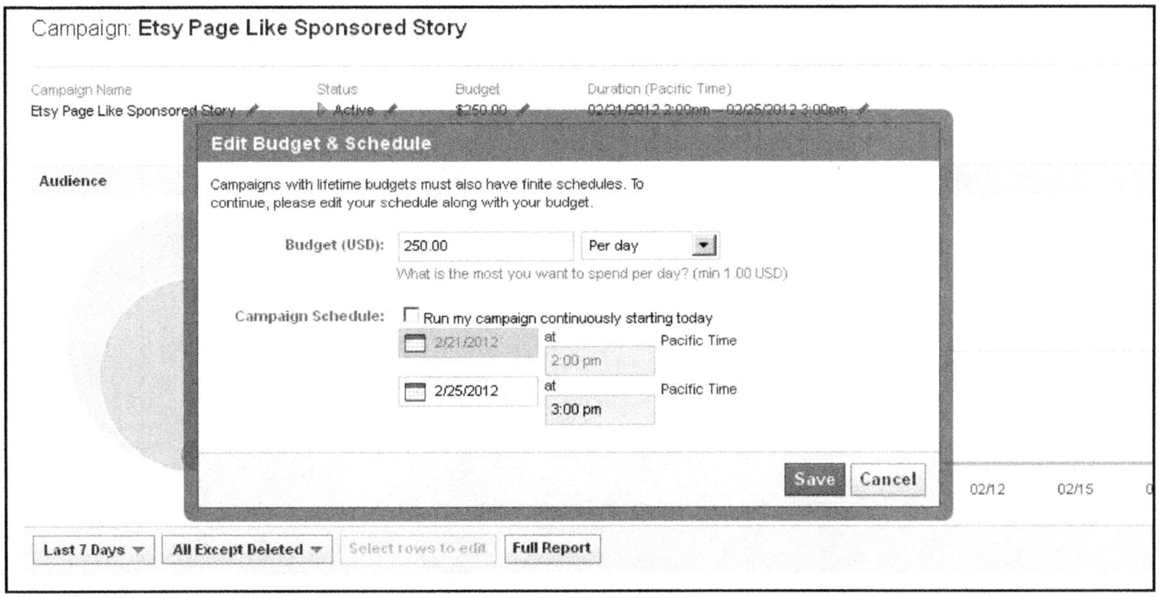

In addition to monitoring your ad spending through Facebook's website, you'll also receive daily summaries via email.

Hedge your advertising "bets"

When you select your budget for an ad, it's always best to choose a small amount at first. Since you can get live feedback on your ad's performance using Facebook's ad manager and the Insights tool, ensure your ad is getting results before committing to a larger investment. It's a simple, prudent strategy: prevent any big losses from unproven ads.

A small amount—perhaps $10 to $50—is a sufficient start. You can invest more once you've discovered that an ad will get results. Remember, an ad loses its effectiveness as your target audience becomes accustomed to seeing it, and the ad begins to blend into the background.

If an ad fares poorly, you'll learn from the experience. You can revisit the drawing board and fashion a new, perhaps more effective ad. If this is the case, simply stop the campaign and start a new one.

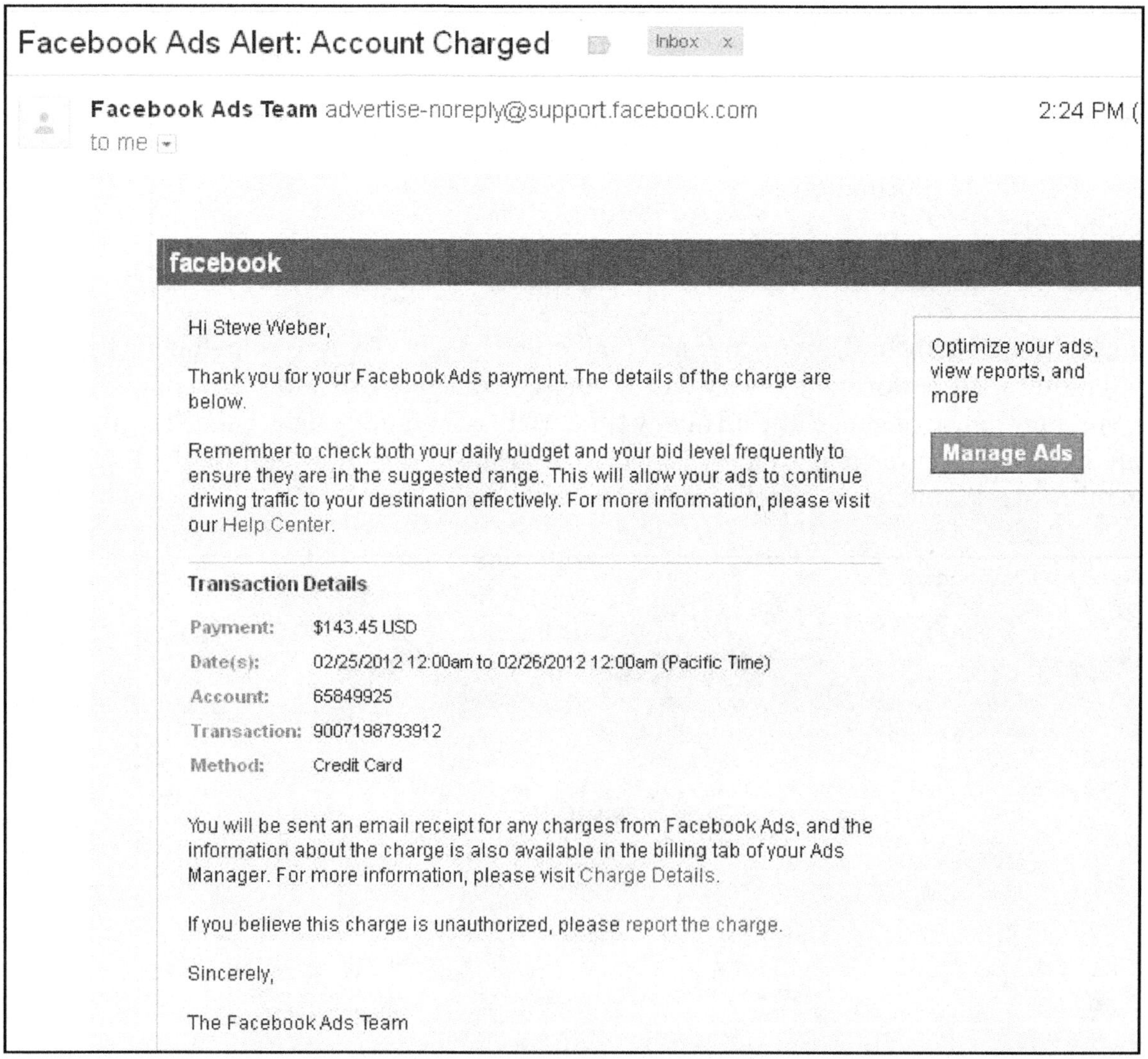

Facebook Ads Alert: Account Charged Inbox x

Facebook Ads Team advertise-noreply@support.facebook.com 2:24 PM (
to me

facebook

Hi Steve Weber,

Thank you for your Facebook Ads payment. The details of the charge are below.

Remember to check both your daily budget and your bid level frequently to ensure they are in the suggested range. This will allow your ads to continue driving traffic to your destination effectively. For more information, please visit our Help Center.

Optimize your ads, view reports, and more

Manage Ads

Transaction Details

Payment:	$143.45 USD
Date(s):	02/25/2012 12:00am to 02/26/2012 12:00am (Pacific Time)
Account:	65849925
Transaction:	9007198793912
Method:	Credit Card

You will be sent an email receipt for any charges from Facebook Ads, and the information about the charge is also available in the billing tab of your Ads Manager. For more information, please visit Charge Details.

If you believe this charge is unauthorized, please report the charge.

Sincerely,

The Facebook Ads Team

Split testing: scheduling ads like a marketing pro

It's a very common tactic for professional marketers to test new campaigns by simultaneously running multiple versions of an ad, each with different art, copy, targeting options or combination of these. This practice, called "split testing," lets you measure the effectiveness of different versions of an ad. The better-performing ads are continued, and the laggards are canceled. Much like using a limited budget to start a new campaign, you'll determine which ad images, copy and targeting work best by analyzing the campaign with Facebook's Ad Manager and Insights tool.

You'll want to invest a small budget toward each version of an ad under the daily budget structure, so this might cost a little more to try from the onset. You'll need to pay for enough exposure of each version of your ad to judge its effectiveness.

Campaign wrap-up and getting it posted

Okay, we're almost ready to post our first Facebook ad. To finish up, simply click the "review ad" button at the bottom of the campaign creation page. You'll arrive at a page that estimates the potential reach of your campaign, as well as a preview of your ad.

Pay careful attention to your preview to ensure that there aren't any typos or image display issues. Also, make sure that you entered the correct budget and payment structure as well; no one wants to be held liable for an extra zero somewhere. After you've verified that your information is correct, you'll be asked to enter your payment information. Once you do this, and it's accepted, you'll receive an email that looks very similar to the one below that acts as a receipt for your purchase.

Facebook Ads Team advertise-noreply@support.facebook.com 1:59 PM (28
to me

facebook

Hi Steve Weber,

Thanks for creating a Facebook Ad or Sponsored Story! Your confirmation is below. Please note that you will only be charged for the impressions or clicks your ad receives. The total charge will not exceed the daily campaign budget you have set.

Remember to create multiple versions of your Facebook Ads. Successful advertisers recommend starting off with 5 to 10 versions of your ads to test which combinations of images and text are most effective.

If you have any questions about your Facebook Ads or Sponsored Stories, please visit our Help Center.

Optimize your ads, view reports, and more

Manage Ads

Ad Preview

Etsy 101: Sell Your Crafts on...

Click "Like" if you love Etsy

Like · Steve Weber likes this.

Campaign: Etsy Page Like Sponsored Story
Daily Budget: $150.00
Start Date: 02/21/2012
End Date: 03/08/2012

As soon as your payment is verified, the Facebook advertising staff will review your ad to ensure it complies with their guidelines, and then it will begin appearing to its targeted audience.

Post campaign analysis and the Ad Manager tool

Within the next few hours and days after you post a campaign, it's very important that you pay close attention to the response your ad gets from viewers. There are two sets of tools you can use to do this.

The first is Facebook's "Insights" tool. This tool is available to anyone with a business page, not just those who buy ads. It's important to review your Page's performance metrics immediately after you purchase an ad, especially if your ad uses your business's Timeline as its "destination." If you aren't seeing a sudden increase in the level of interaction with your page, as well as other stats revealed on the Insights tool, you'll need to reconsider your ad's approach.

Here's a view of the Insights tool:

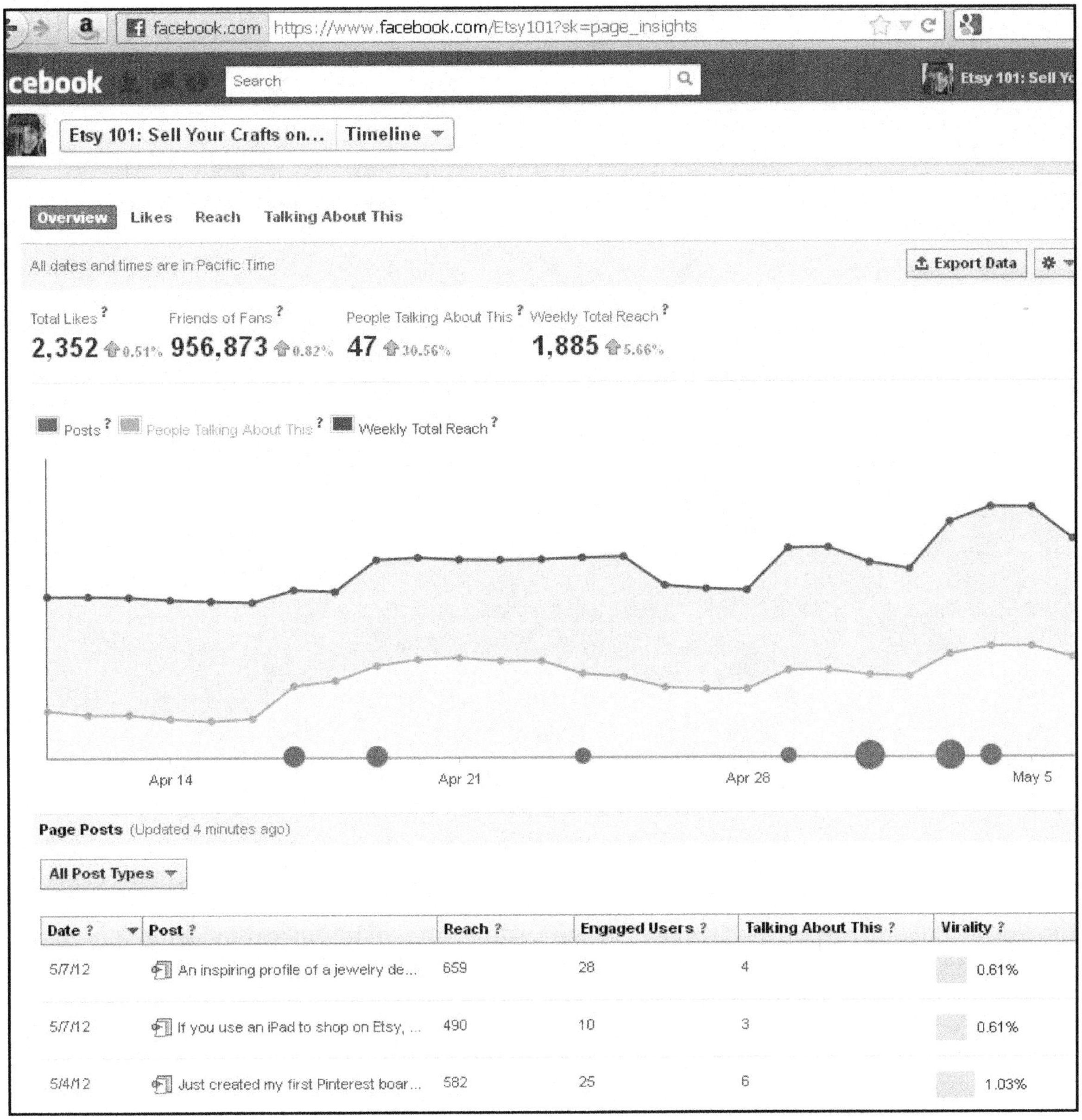

The second set of tools is the Facebook manager's "Home page" and "Reports" tabs.

To access the ad manager, simply go to the Facebook advertising home page and look for the "Manage your existing ads" link near the bottom of the page. The ad manager is where you'll be doing most of your interaction with Facebook's advertising platform after posting your first campaign. Here's a tab-by-tab breakdown and what each page in the ad manager can do for you.

The Ad Manager home page

As you can see, the Ad Manager home page provides a full list of your ad campaigns and is a convenient way to check their performance. You'll also notice a pie graph showing the reach metrics for your ads, a line graph depicting the interactions viewers have had with your ads, and a table that shows the numerical statistics that Facebook tracks for your ads' performances.

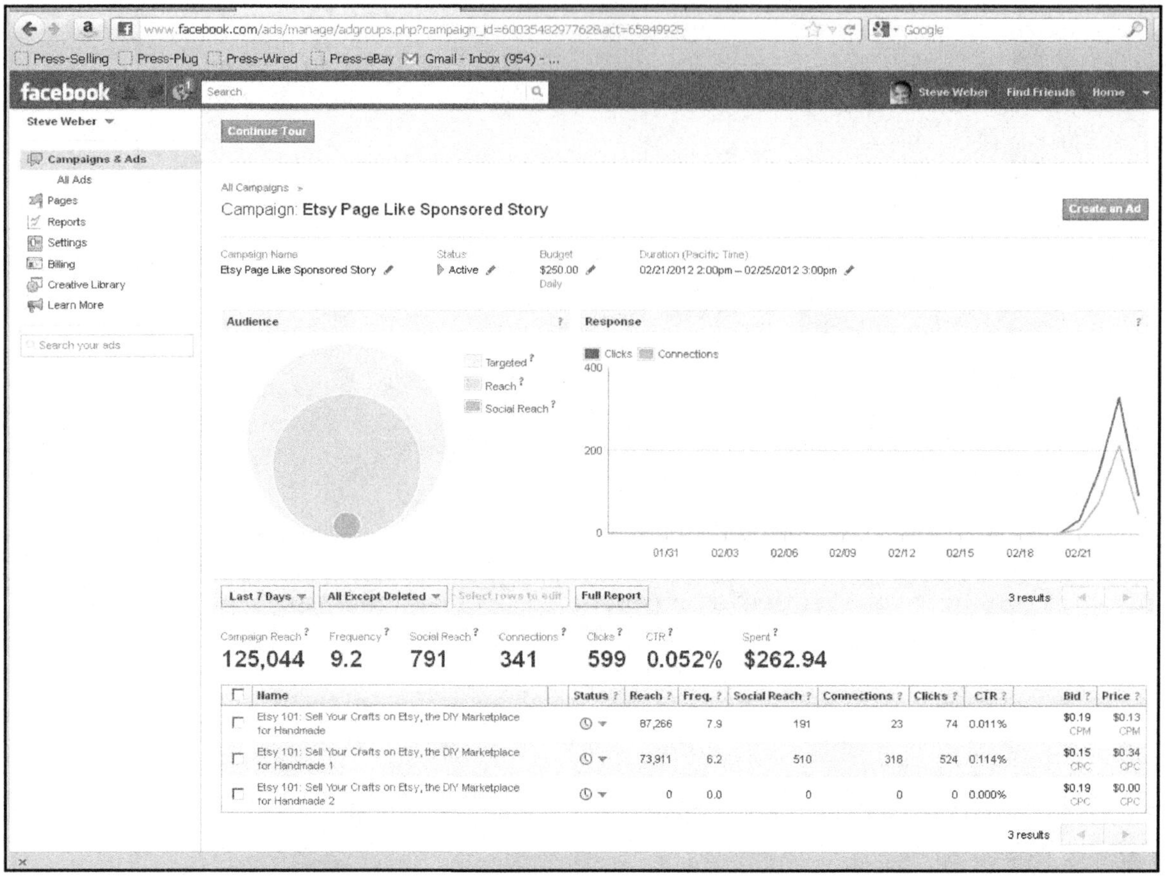

A row of buttons directly underneath the two graphs will also allow you sort and show campaigns according to different categories, such as "active, paused or completed campaigns" or show statistics accumulated during specific time frames. You can also click the name of an individual campaign in the lower table to see just the information that pertains to that particular campaign, and a preview of what it looks like, as well.

Reading the audience pie graph

The pie graph you'll see on the Ad Manager home page is an easy and quick-to-read way to see how your campaign is reaching its potential audience. It's made of three overlapping circles, each intended to represent a different "reach" metric. The largest represents the maximum number of users that meet your targeting requirements. The second represents the number of them that have currently seen your ad. The third, and smallest, shows the current "social reach," or the number of potential viewers whose friends have interacted with your page.

Reading the 'response' graph

The response graph is a simple two-line graph that shows the interactions viewers of your ad have had with it. The blue line simply shows the number of clicks that your ad has drawn. The green line shows the "connections" that your ad has created for your page. A "connection" is the number of Likes your page has drawn, or RSVPs your event has gained within 24 hours after a viewer has seen your ad.

Understanding the chart data

There are several fields in the chart at the bottom of the home page that represent several different statistics:

- **Name** - The name of the specific campaign, used only for identification purposes
- **Status** - Shows whether the ad is running, completed or paused
- **Reach** - Reveals how many people have seen your ad during the selected time period (not to be confused with impressions in the similar chart in the reports tab)
- **Freq** - The frequency, the number of times your ad has been seen per viewer
- **Social reach** - The numerical data that goes into the circle graph above the chart which represents the number of viewers that have seen that their friends have interacted with your page
- **Clicks** - The number of clicks your ad has generated
- **CTR** - The percentage of viewers that have clicked on your ad (Don't be concerned if this number seems low. Any number over a tenth of a percent is excellent, and these are typically in the hundredth of a percent range.)
- **Bid** - This number reflects the maximum that you've said you'll pay for either 1,000 impressions or per click
- **Price** - This number represents what you're actually being charged per thousand impressions or clicks

By using these numbers and graphs to analyze your campaign, you can easily judge which campaigns are performing efficiently. Combined with these the Insights Tool, these pages should help you decide which ads are working best during a split test, or if they are effective in general.

Pages tab: The pages tab is very simple. Clicking it will display the business pages that you currently own, and it offers some very basic information that also appears in the Insights tool.

Reports tab: The reports tab is another tool in the ad manager that will help you analyze your campaign's effectiveness. It provides a few different types of more detailed reports, which you can export into a spreadsheet if you wish. With the "schedule reports" sub-tab, you can also have reports automatically generated on a regular basis and have an email notification sent to you when this happens.

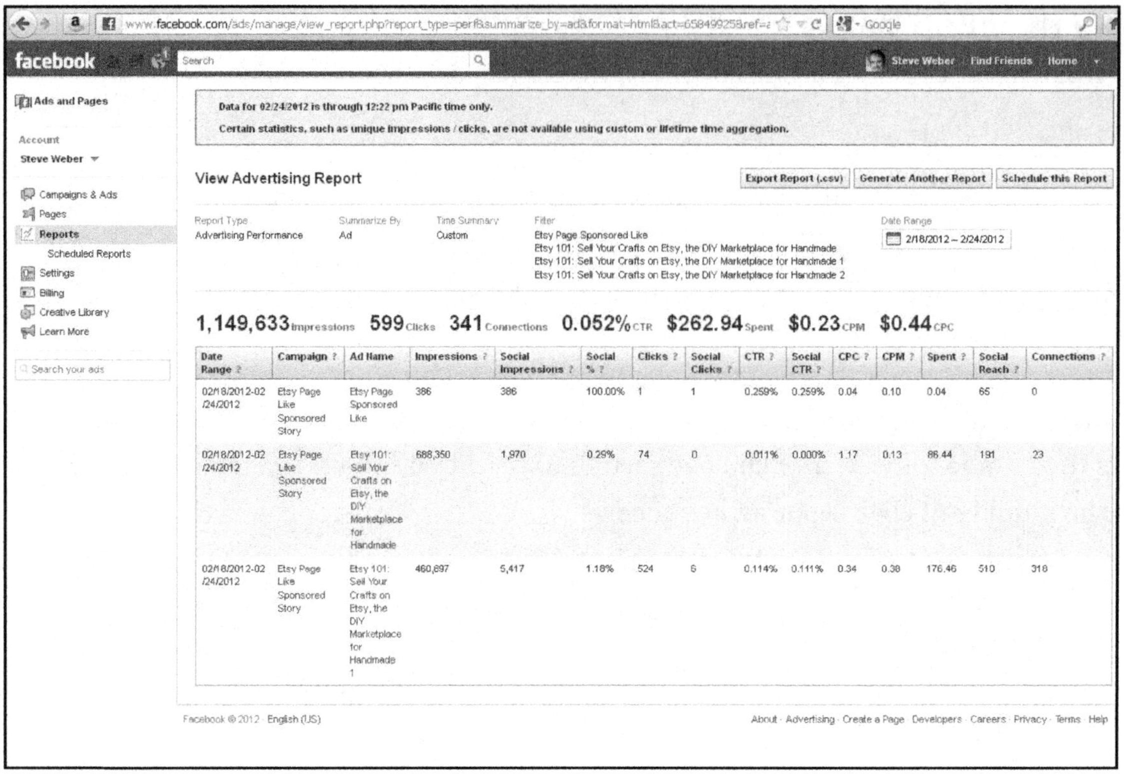

Much of the information that will be produced in these reports is advanced-level marketing data. The types of reports that you can export include:

Advertising performance: The advertising performance report offers very similar data to what you'll find on the home page of the Ad Manager with a few different fields. They don't include any terminology or concepts that we haven't already discussed, so you should be able to decipher what each field represents.

Responder demographics: The responder demographic report gives you a deep level of information on the individuals who are viewing your ad. This report is designed to help you find out specialized and deep information regarding the viewers of an ad, and which types are responding the most.

Conversions by impression: This report shows you a list of different metrics that represent the relationship between the time the user sees the ad and when they act on it. It's designed to show you how many times typical users see the ad before they click on it or Like your page. This is designed to show you how effective the art and copy is.

Inline interactions: This report shows you detailed information regarding the different interactions viewers have with your page after clicking your ad. This includes timeline photo views, video plays, comments, etc.

Settings tab: The settings tab simply allows you to change and view the information that you and your business have on file with Facebook's ad platform. It has no effect on or relevance to your ads or their performance.

Billing tab: This is another tab dedicated to clerical information. This is where you can view your billing history and receipts.

Creative library: The creative library is collection of all the creative assets that you've used in your ads. This can be extremely helpful if you access Facebook from different computers and need to access your ad materials on different machines. You can also add new creative assets for future campaigns with this tool.

Power editor tab: The power editor tab is an advanced feature that requires a specific browser to use. If you're a highly technical individual, it might be worth your time to learn it, as it gives you an even more streamlined way to post ads quickly.

By now, you should have a good understanding of the different types of effective strategies you can use within Facebook's paid ad platform, as well as how to analyze and improve your campaigns. We discussed the different types of paid Facebook ads, such as standard ads and sponsored stories, and gave tips on creating your ad and selecting its targets. Finally, we reviewed the ad management tools offered by Facebook.

11 ▶ FACEBOOK PLATFORM, OTHER APPLICATIONS

The platform is the name Facebook has given to the facility that allows developers to create applications that run on Facebook. Applications are programs. Developers have created thousands of applications that allow people to do all sorts of things on Facebook. For example, you can use applications to play games, sort your photos, and record where you have been in your life on an interactive world map.

Of course Facebook has its own applications. Events and Photos are two examples. But the people who run Facebook have decided that opening up the site to other developers can only make it more attractive.

Using applications to promote your business

There are three basic approaches to creating and using applications to promote your business.

Develop your own application: This requires considerable time and programming expertise. Most small organizations do not have the budget or the personnel to take on this task.

Hire someone to develop an application: You don't have to be a computer genius to do this, but you do need to come up with a clever, engaging idea and then find someone with the expertise to translate your idea into code. A company like Facebookster (www.facebookster.com) will develop an application for as little as $1,000 in about two weeks. Other application developers include:

- Art & Logic (www.artlogic.com)
- Notice Technologies (www.noticetechnologies.com)
- Ayoka (www.ayokasystems.com)
- Invoke(www.invokemedia.com)

The problem with hiring someone to develop an application is that your application will be competing with thousands of others on Facebook. Unless you and your developer come up with something really special, you will probably not get the kind of attention you would like to have. You might end up spending a lot of money and then have little to show for it.

Pay to place ads on applications developed by other people: Of course, there is still a cost involved in this option, but unless you plan a mammoth ad campaign, this approach should be considerably more manageable than developing your own application or hiring someone to develop one for you. The good thing about this option is that, within certain limits, you can spend as much or as little as you want on advertising. For most small businesses and other organizations, this is the most practical way to advertise on applications.

Advertising on applications

If you build your own application or hire someone to build it, you have a lot of control over the ads you display. Of course, your ads can't be obscene or objectionable in other ways, and you have to stay away from forbidden products like tobacco. (To review Facebook's ad rules, see www.facebook.com/ad_guidelines.php.) But apart from that, you're in charge of your own ads. Some applications use clever devices to ensure that users will view their ads for a certain length of time. For example, a game application might display an ad for a certain number of seconds in between rounds. Players can't move on to the next round until the ad has run its course. If you take this approach, you need to be careful not to make users so annoyed that they stop coming back to your applications.

If you decide to advertise on someone else's application, you need to choose the application carefully. A number of advertising networks are available to help you place your ads on the most relevant applications. Some of the more widely used networks are:

- AdBrite (www.adbrite.com)
- SocialMedia (www.socialmedia.com)
- Rock You (www.rockyou.com)
- Adonomics (www.adonomics.com)
- Lookery (www.lookery.com)

Some of these networks allow you to use targeting criteria that are different from those offered by Facebook. For example, AdBrite allows you to define your audience by income level and ethnicity, two options that Facebook does not provide. Options like these might enable you to target your ads more precisely than you can with standard Facebook advertising.

Adding apps to your page

To add an app to your page or account, you will need to enter the name of it in the search bar at the top of your Facebook page. Click the magnifying glass and then click on the Search Filter Apps on the left sidebar, and then select from the list of results.

If you would just like to browse the applications that are available, visit the App Center. It is listed in the left sidebar of your home page, and also found at www.facebook.com/applications.

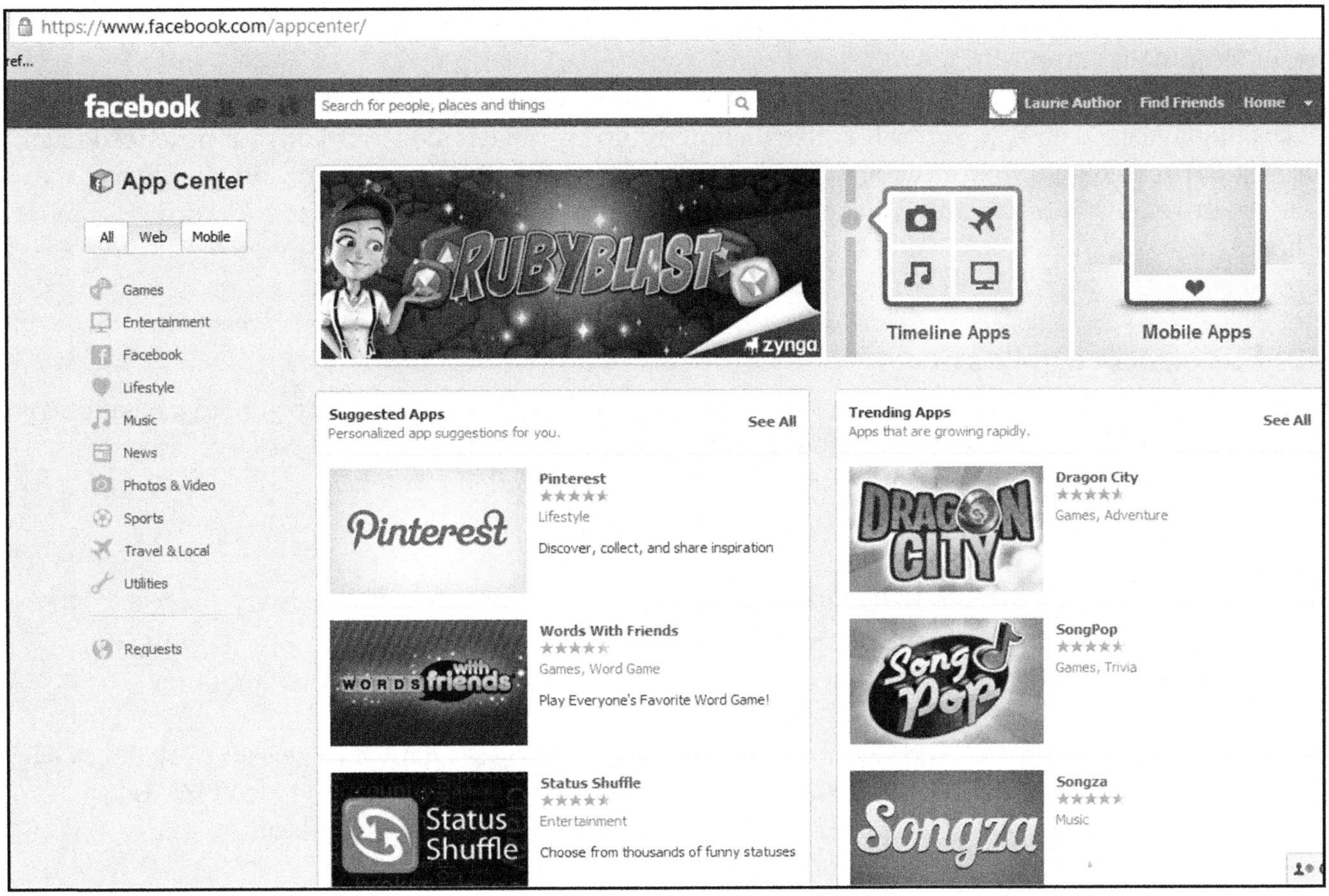

On the left sidebar of the App Center page, you can click on the box for All, Web and Mobile apps, respectively. Below that you have your choice of categories such as Games, Entertainment, Facebook, Lifestyle, Music, etc.

In the middle of the app center page is a box of "Suggested Apps" that Facebook thinks you may like. Next to that is a box of Trending Apps that are popular and growing rapidly on Facebook. You can also click on the box to see apps that are specifically Mobile Games and those that are made to be used on the timeline view of Facebook pages.

If you don't see anything that looks interesting, scroll further down the page and click on the tabs in the next box for Top Rated, Trending and Grossing Apps. To gain access to some applications, you may have to give the application access to your profile information, photos, your friends' info, and other content. This might seem like an invasion of your privacy and the privacy of your friends, and some Facebook members have complained about it. Facebook has tried to assure members that their information is being used only by the application itself, not for any marketing purposes. For example, if you use the popular Word Challenge application, you will see your high score, name and photo along with the high scores, names and photos of your friends who have played the game. Application developers know that if they use personal information like this for spamming they will be banned from Facebook.

When you view some applications, you will see a page giving you more information about that app, including a brief description of what you can do with the app, some photos, and even how many people currently use the app. You can also click on Visit Website or Visit App Page; it is from the App Page that you can commit to the application, although each page uses a different lingo, such as Go to App, Play Game, or simply Visit App.

Once you have used an app, you will notice it showing up on the left sideboard of your newsfeed page, under Apps. If you change your mind and decide you don't want the application on your profile or page, you can easily remove it from your privacy settings and the drop down arrow next to the word "Home" on your home page.

Other Facebook applications

Up to this point, we have focused on the basics of using Facebook, especially to promote a business or other organization. But there are lots of other cool things you can do on Facebook. Now we'll focus on three applications that you might want to try out: Mobile, Notes and Marketplace.

Facebook Mobile: Connecting on the Run

Facebook has developed a convenient application that allows you to access your profile with your mobile phone and use many features of the site the way you normally would on your computer.

To use Facebook Mobile, you need a phone with an Internet browser, and your service provider needs to support the application. In the United States, Facebook Mobile Web is supported by AT&T, Boost, Nextel, Sprint, Verizon, Helio and Virgin USA. In Canada, it is supported by Bell Mobility, Aliant, Solo, Fido, Rogers, TELUS, SaskTel, Virgin Mobile Canada, and MTS.

To begin using Facebook Mobile, go to the app's homepage by searching for it. This will take you to the main Facebook Mobile screen. From there you can click on Get the App. Enter your country and mobile phone number; Facebook will send a link to your mobile phone number which you can use to activate your account. Once you do this, you can receive messages, friend requests, wall posts, and status updates on your phone.

Facebook looks a bit different on your phone, but it still offers you most of what you are accustomed to seeing. The main headings on Facebook Mobile are:

- **News Feed:** Read your news feed, post status updates or photos on your wall, and use Facebook's GPS to Check In and tell your Friends where you are.
- **Messages:** Check your Facebook messages.
- **Nearby:** See a list of your friends' latest check-ins.
- **Events:** See a list of events you have indicated you will attend.
- **Find Friends:** Find friends from your phone list as well as your existing friends list by suggesting friends of friends.

You can also view your Friends list, your Pages and Groups you belong to, as well as access the app center and use some the apps you have previously downloaded if they can be used with mobile devices.

Your Facebook settings and the Help Center are also accessible from the mobile app.

Facebook Notes: Letting your friends know what's on your mind

Notes are like blogs. They allow you to write about whatever is on your mind. They are a way to publish something to your page that is longer than a Status Update, and a good way to attach some significance or importance to whatever is in the Note.

You can access the notes application by clicking on the notepad icon on the left sidebar of any Facebook screen. You will see any notes your friends have added to their profiles and any comments their friends have made about the notes. If you have created any Pages, you will see an option for Pages' Notes. You will also have options for My Drafts, Notes About Me, and My Notes.

Click on Write a Note at the top of the screen to compose a note of your own.

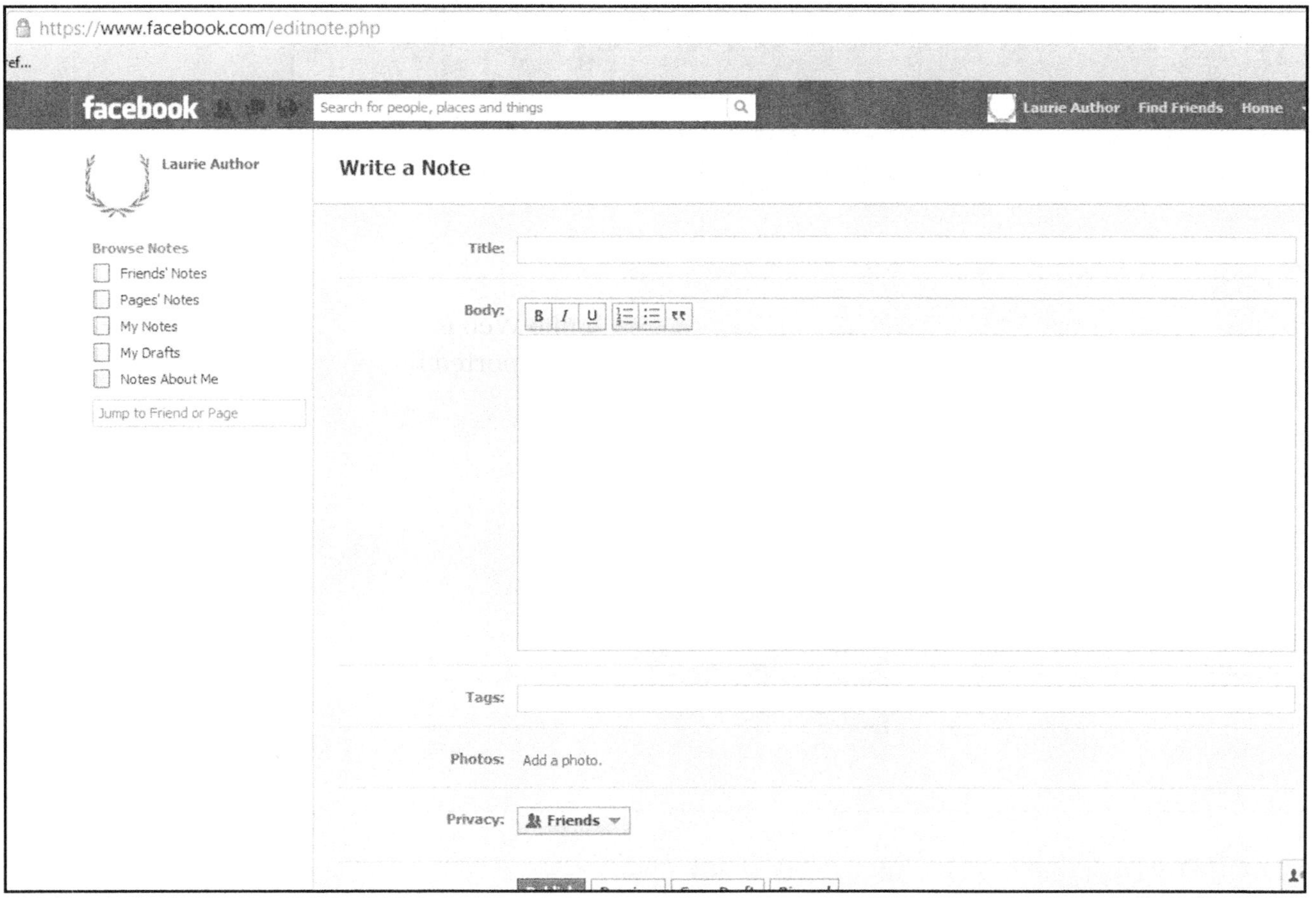

Type a title for your note in the title box and then start composing your note. You have a few formatting options for your note, such as bolding, italicizing or underlining characters, as well as bullet lists and a couple of others. There is no standard length for a note. In deciding how long your note should be, think about how much time your friends are likely to spend reading it. You can also assign tags to the note and add photos.

When you have finished your note, click Preview to see what it will look like. If you're satisfied with it, click Publish to share it with your friends. The Note Privacy box lets you place restrictions on who will be able to see your note.

Facebook Marketplace, powered by oodle

Marketplace is an online version of classified ads, similar to the popular site CraigsList. You can use it to buy or sell things, find an apartment, look for a job, or promote your event. Marketplace is organized by location, so the ads you post will be seen by people in your area.

Use the search feature on the App Center page to find it.

From the Marketplace home page, you will be asked to give your geographical location; this is so that the ads you see are pertinent to your area.

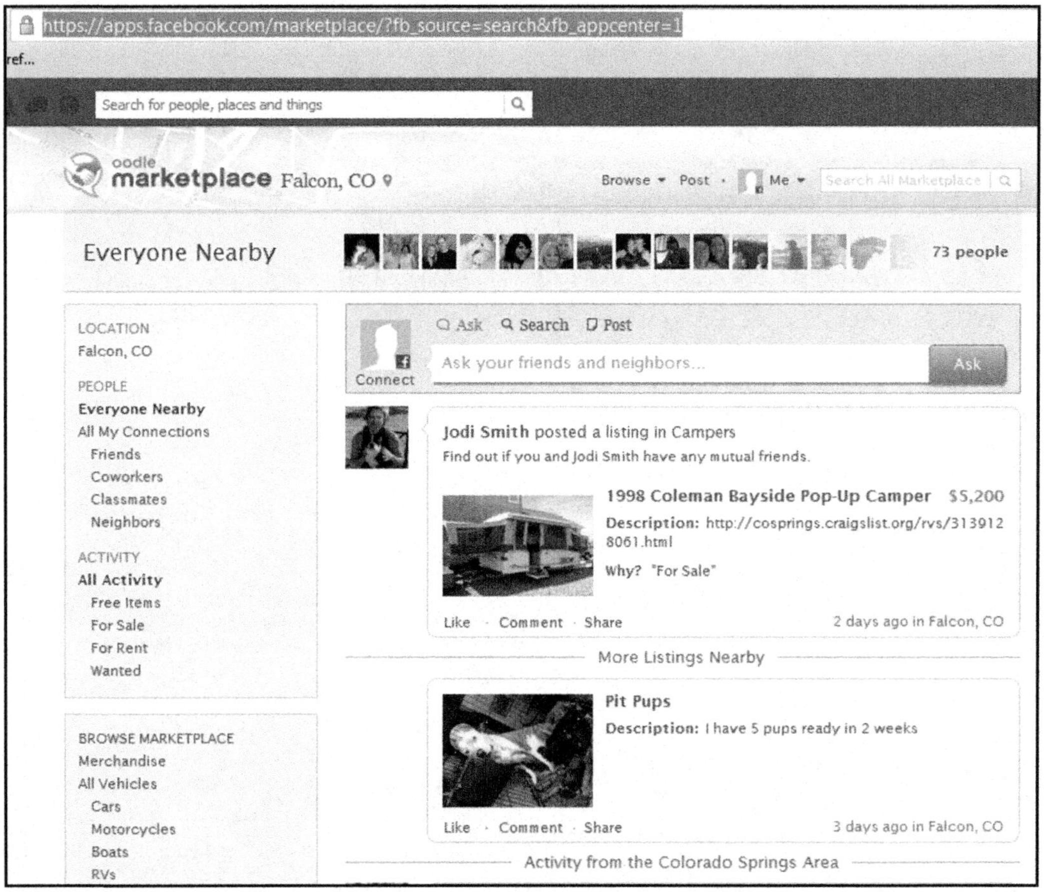

The Marketplace home page has nine areas of ads:

- Community
- Houses
- Jobs
- Merchandise
- Pets
- Rentals
- Services
- Tickets

- Vehicle

Many of these categories have subcategories. For example, the subcategories for vehicles are:

- Airplanes
- ATVs
- Boats
- Cars
- Commercial Trucks
- Everything Else
- Heavy Equipment
- Motorcycles
- Parts & Accessories
- Power Sports
- RVs Snowmobiles
- Storage

Click on a subcategory to see the listings. Each listing will have basic information. For example, the listing for an apartment might include the general location, rent and a few words of description. If something looks interesting, click on the listing for more information. You will see a more detailed description of what is being offered and the name and photo of the person who posted the ad. You will also be able to contact the person from this page.

To post an item on Marketplace, click on Post at the top of the Marketplace home page.

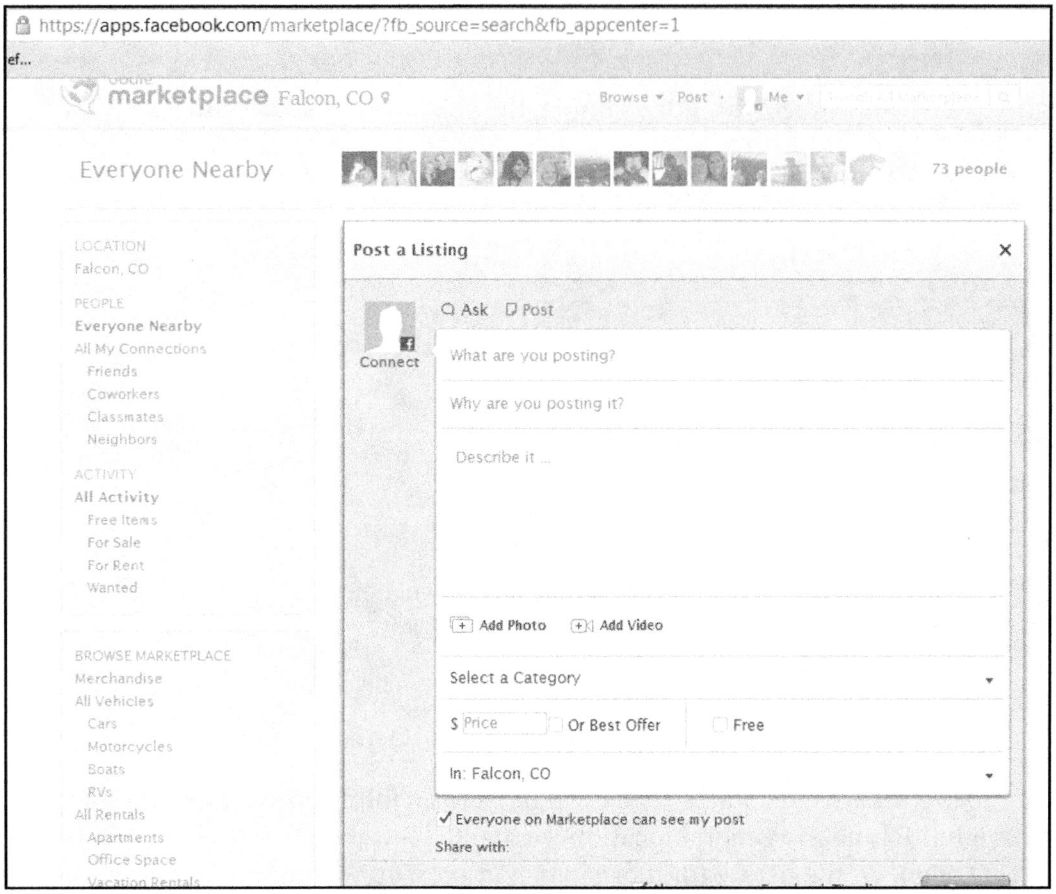

You will be asked to fill in the following information:

- What are you posting?
- Why are you posting it?
- Describe it. (Here you also have an opportunity to Add Photo or Video of your item.)
- Select a Category
- Price

Your geographical location will be shown at the bottom of the listing. You can check boxes for two posting options:

- Everyone on Marketplace can see my post
- Also post to my Facebook Timeline

Then, click the orange Post box. For your ad to be posted, you have to allow Marketplace to display your name and profile picture.

Index

7-Eleven, 76
Acquaintances, 35
ad bids, 109
ad campaigns, 85
Ad Center, 88
ad copy, 94
ad creation tool, 89
ad destination, 89
Ad Manager, 107
ad reports, 107
AdBrite, 114
Adonomic, 114
advanced targeting, 100
advertising audience, 97
advertising budgets, 103
advertising location, 98
advertising payment, 102
advertising performance, 110
advertising reach, 109
advertising text, 94
advertising with applications, 114
age targeting, 99
App Center, 115
Apple Mail, 40
applications, 113
badges for websites, blogs, 67
blue menu bar, 33
Calendar, 73
campaigns, advertising, 85
chatting, 34
click-through rate (CTR), 84
Close Friends, 35
Colt, Beth, 18
communicating privately, 41
Connections, 100
Conversions by impression, 110
cost-per-click (CPC), 102
cost-per-thousand impressions (CPM), 102
creative library, 111
Crème-Delicious, 13
CTR (Click-through Rate), 84
Davis, Ben, 16
demographics, 8
Down-facing arrow, 35
editing photos, 49
email invitations, 40
email notifications, 34
event, advertising, 92
Events, 10, 73
Events, creating, 74
Facebook advertising, 31
Facebook Platform, 9, 31, 113
Facemash, 8
Family, 35
filters, 35
finding friends, 39
Friends icon, 36
Gents Place, 16
Getting Started page, 28
Globe icon, 34
Google Analytics, 23
Groups, 10
Groups, joining, 51
Home page, 33
impressions, 84
Inedible Jewelry, 21
Inline interactions, 110
Insights, 68, 106
interests, 99
Like box plugin, 67
Like button, 85
Local Friends, 35
logos, Page, 60
Lookery, 114

Map pin icon, 36
Marketplace, 118
Messages icon, 34
Microsoft Outlook, 40
mobile users, 116
News Feed, 36
Notes, 117
Outlook Express, 40
Pages, 30
Pages, creating, 55
paid advertising, 79
Partain, Jessica, 21
Partain, Susan, 21
Patangay, Sandy, 13
personal profile, 10
photo albums, 48
photo sharing, 47
photos, deleting, 49
postal quality, 70
privacy settings, 37, 41, 43
profile picture, 29
responder demographics, 110
Restricted Lists, 35
Rock You, 114
RSS feed, 34
School Friends, 35
sex targeting, 99
Skype, 39
social reach, 109
SocialMedia, 114
split testing, 105
Sponsored Stories, 85
sponsored story, creating, 90
standard ads, 90
status updates, 37
tagging photos, 49
targeting, advertising, 31
Text Message, 34
text messaging, 34
Update Status, 36
uploading photos, 48
video calling, 34
virality, 70
Windows Contacts, 40
Woods Hole Inn, 18
Work Friends, 35
YouTube, 68
Zuckerberg, Mark, 7

Printed in Dunstable, United Kingdom

91223995R00071